The Wannsee Conference and the Final Solution

ALSO BY MARK ROSEMAN

A Past in Hiding:
Memory and Survival in Nazi Germany

The

WANNSEE CONFERENCE

and the

FINAL SOLUTION

A RECONSIDERATION

MARK ROSEMAN

PICADOR

A METROPOLITAN BOOK

HENRY HOLT AND COMPANY

NEW YORK

www.picadorusa.com

Picador® is a U.S. registered trademark and is used by Henry Holt and Company
under license from Pan Books Limited.

For information on Picador Reading Group Guides, as well as ordering,
please contact the Trade Marketing department at St. Martin's Press.
Phone: 1-800-221-7945 extension 763
Fax: 212-677-7456
E-mail: trademarketing@stmartins.com

Library of Congress Cataloging-in-Publication Data

Roseman, Mark.
    The Wannsee Conference and the final solution : a reconsideration / Mark
Roseman.
        p. cm.
    Includes bibliographical references and index.
    ISBN 0-312-42234-2
    I. Wannsee-Konferenz (1942: Berlin, Germany) 2. Holocaust, Jewish
(1939–1945) 3. War criminals—Germany. I. Title.

D804.3. R6627 2002
940.53'18—dc21   2001056262

First published in the United States by Henry Holt and Company

FOR
ANN LARABEE

CONTENTS

THE WANNSEE CONFERENCE
AND THE FINAL SOLUTION

"Perhaps the Most
Shameful Document"

It was in March 1947, as they were collecting information
for the Nuremberg trials, that staff of the American prosecutor made the discovery.[1] Stamped *"Geheime Reichssache"*—
"Secret Reich matter"—and tucked away in a German Foreign
Office folder were the minutes of a meeting. The meeting
had involved fifteen top Nazi civil servants, SS officials, and
party representatives and had taken place on January 20,
1942, in a grand Berlin villa on the shores of Lake Wannsee.
The Americans had stumbled across the only surviving copy
of the minutes, number sixteen out of an original thirty.

The minutes, or Wannsee Protocol (as they soon came to
be known in deference to the German term for minutes),
consist largely of a presentation by Reinhard Heydrich, head
of the Nazi Security Service (SD) and chief of the German
Security Police. Heydrich surveys the measures taken toward

Jews up to 1941, tallies the number of Jews remaining in Axis, occupied, neutral, and enemy Europe, and outlines a plan to "evacuate" them to the East. There is an extended discussion of how to deal with the half Jew, the quarter Jew, the Jew married to the Gentile, the war-decorated Jew. While Heydrich's proposal is to comb Europe from West to East, the representative for the German administration of Poland makes a plea for the program to begin in his territory. They had so many useless Jews in Poland. Despite using the language of evacuation, the minutes unmistakably contain a plan for genocide, formulated in sober bureaucratic language, deliberated on in civilized surroundings in a once cosmopolitan suburb of Berlin.

In 1947 the man in charge of prosecuting the German ministries was Robert Kempner, a former German (Jewish) civil servant who had immigrated to the United States in the 1930s. When the protocol was discovered, Kempner rushed to his boss, Brigadier General Telford Taylor, to show him what he had found. "Is such a thing possible?" Taylor asked.[2] Both men knew they had unearthed "perhaps the most shameful document of modern history."[3] Indeed, there has never been a bleaker rendition of the orderly governance of murder. To this day the Wannsee Protocol remains the most emblematic and programmatic statement of the Nazi way of genocide.

Yet the protocol is a deeply mysterious document. It seems to capture the precise moment when the Nazis decided to eliminate the Jews. Small wonder that the prosecutors believed they had found the Rosetta stone of Nazi murder or that the Wannsee Protocol still figures as such in the popular imagination.[4] But historians have long argued that the document cannot be what it seems. For one thing, Hitler was not at the conference, and those present were too junior to decide on genocide. Above all, the timing seems wrong. The mass murder of Soviet Jews had begun half a year earlier. Polish Jews had been gassed at Chelmno since early December 1941. The Belzec extermination camp was in the midst of construction. So what then was the purpose of the gathering at Wannsee?

Most historians discount the idea that Wannsee represented a radical new plan and interpret the meeting rather as an exercise in self-aggrandizement on the part of its convener, Reinhard Heydrich. If they are correct, the protocol's historical significance is simply that it offers a clear picture of matters long decided elsewhere. Yet such an interpretation, while understandable in view of the shootings and gassings already under way, does little to explain Heydrich's claim that the meeting was necessary to prepare a "comprehensive solution"—or, as it says elsewhere, the "coming final solution"—of the Jewish question; or the protocol's assumption that at the time of the meeting that solution had not yet begun. Most historians would probably agree with Eberhard Jäckel, therefore, that "the most remarkable thing about the Wannsee conference is that we do not know why it took place."[5]

But the protocol's macabre mystery goes deeper still. Even if we knew why the meeting was called, would that render it any more intelligible? Would we then be able to account for its mixture of procedure and prejudice, sober planning and ideologically motivated murder? Could we ever make sense of the devilish parody of administrative precision, delineating between the quarter Jew (to be vetted), the half Jew (to be sterilized or worse), or the full Jew (to be "evacuated")? How was it possible, in other words, on a snowy January day in Berlin to deliberate so calmly and carefully about genocide?

The Wannsee Protocol is emblematic of the Holocaust not just in its methodical blueprint for murder. On the one hand, the protocol exists, its authenticity undeniable, its leaden matter-of-factness as unanswerable as it is unfathomable.[6] It reminds us that the Holocaust is the best-documented mass murder in history. Bureaucracy was its hallmark, after all. Despite Nazi efforts to destroy the evidence, huge quantities of records were collected after the war, first by the legal teams of the various postwar tribunals, later by historians. During the war the Allies eavesdropped on German communications, and now their transcripts, too, are accessible. After 1945, thousands of testimonies were given in courtroom hearings and conversations with historians that together have opened up, as documents alone never could, the inner workings of the Nazi system of murder—forced labor, extermination camps, and death marches.

Yet when it comes to understanding why and how the process was undertaken, the documentation is much less complete. Key papers have been destroyed. Many of the files belonging to the Reich Security Main Office (RSHA), the body headed by Reinhard Heydrich—the man who called the Wannsee Conference—have not been found and probably no longer exist. At the very top of the Nazi system, there were no files anyway. Hitler never put commands on Jewish matters in writing; Himmler, too, was extraordinarily cautious. Moreover, the decision to carry out mass extermination in the middle of a major war is so strange, so counterintuitive that a paper trail that would otherwise suffice to certify the parentage of an idea or a policy is here not enough. That is why the present book opens not with a reconstruction of the conference itself but with the discovery of the protocol, as a reminder that what we have is a document, not a camera-eye view. Why did Heydrich select this particular group of participants? What was his agenda? Why did his invitees attend and what did they say that is not in the minutes? On all of these things, we have to speculate.

The gaps in the record, but even more the questions Wannsee raises, force us to cast our net far wider than the meeting itself. In particular, the protocol's implication that the groundwork for the Final Solution had still not been prepared in January 1942 poses with peculiar force a question hovering over the entire history of the Holocaust: Was the descent into genocide the result of a long-established plan?

This question is difficult to answer partly because of the ambiguous character of Hitler's command. In general terms and particularly in relation to the Final Solution it is often unclear how binding and precise his orders were. Moreover, the Nazi war on Jews in the nine years between Hitler's seizure of power and the Wannsee Conference was characterized by a paradoxical combination of constant commitment and changing purpose that is very hard to interpret.

During the 1970s and early 1980s historians were particularly sensitive to these questions of coherence and intention. Some readers will know of the debates between the "intentionalists" and the "functionalists" (sometimes referred to as structuralists).[7] The former emphasized the clarity of Hitler's plans and his control over both people and events. The latter saw Hitler as less decided and less interventionist and believed it was his subordinates' struggle for power in a chaotic political system that tipped the regime over the edge. The research generated in the context of these debates was enormously valuable, but in the process Wannsee became more, not less, of a puzzle.

The problem was not the polarization of interpretations per se. Most historians felt free to take the middle ground.[8] The best work came from "moderate functionalists" who acknowledged Hitler was not always sure what he wanted and often not in full control but who concluded that in the end it was his finger on the button.[9] In such accounts Hitler crossed the Rubicon in July, August, or September

1941. The Wannsee Conference's meaning and timing thus remained elusive. Moreover, the conceptual framework of the intentionalist-functionalist debate bedeviled even the halfway positions. Insofar as there was a clear intention, it was Hitler's; insofar as there was wider participation, that was attributed to "secondary" motives not in themselves genocidal: some authors—none more influential than Raul Hilberg—emphasized the blind obedience of a bureaucracy; others, following Hans Mommsen and Martin Broszat, foregrounded the pulls and pushes of a deformed political system.[10] One does not have to subscribe to Daniel Goldhagen's view of a unique German "eliminatory antisemitism" to agree that such motives for participation are wanting as an explanation for the trajectory and outlook of the men around the Wannsee table.[11]

Over the last decade and a half, new research on the Holocaust has made Wannsee easier to place within the wider project of genocide. Writers such as Saul Friedländer and Ian Kershaw have provided subtle and penetrating accounts of the balance between leadership and followers, control and improvisation that make the mixture of planfulness and planlessness easier to grasp.[12] Recent work by Ulrich Herbert and Peter Longerich, among others, has helped to rediscover the shared values and ideology of Hitler and followers, values not initially genocidal but without which Wannsee could never have happened.[13] Finally, and perhaps most pertinent, the last few years have seen regional studies of the Holocaust in Poland and the former Soviet Union, many of them by younger German historians such as Christoph Dieckmann, Christian Gerlach, Peter Klein, Dieter Pohl, and Thomas Sandkühler, that draw on the vast amount of material hitherto locked up in Soviet bloc archives and that fill some of the gaps in the files of the Nazi leaders.[14] As a result of this work we can see that in a curious feedback process, in some respects not unfamiliar from government policy on other matters and in other places—but horrifically out of place here—the deed of murder begat the idea of genocide as much as the other way around. Wannsee emerges as an important act of closure in the process of turning mass murder into genocide.

This book therefore proceeds with two chapters that set the scene for Wannsee. The first sketches the mixture of strong leadership and hesitancy, energy and chaos, purposefulness and apparent lack of direction that characterized the drift toward genocide in the years up to 1941. The second examines more closely the evidence for a clear decision on the Final Solution in the months leading up to the Wannsee Conference. The remaining two chapters look at the conference itself and its aftermath. In all this, there is, of course, one huge omission. There is nothing here about the victims of this process. Instead, my aim is to paint a picture of how, on January 20, 1942, fifteen serious, intelligent men met to give their assent to genocide.

2

MEIN KAMPF TO MASS MURDER,
1919–41

THE RHETORIC OF EXTERMINATION

The close parallels between Hitler's threats in the 1920s and the Jews' eventual fate in the 1940s might well suggest that the Wannsee Protocol was, in effect, merely a digest of *Mein Kampf*. But the journey to Wannsee is more complicated and ambiguous than that. Hitler's writings in the 1920s certainly show him obsessed with the "Jewish problem," far more so than by Bolshevism or Marxism. Other groups, too, fell foul of Hitler's racial vision—syphilitics, alcoholics, and criminals should all, he argued, be isolated and sterilized, perhaps even "amputated" from German society[1]—but only the Jews were seen as conspiring against the nation. Considered a racial rather than a religious enemy, they could not be redeemed by conversion to Christianity. They were a rootless force seeking to undermine Germany from within and without through the twin agencies of international Bolshevism and international finance capital. From the early 1920s until his death, Hitler remained wedded to the idea that "Juda" was "the plague of the world" and that Germany's future health depended on eradicating it.[2]

Hitler's language is extraordinarily violent and bloodthirsty, filled with metaphors of plague and parasite. The Jew was variously a maggot, a bloodsucking spider, a rat, a harmful bacillus, or a vampire.[3] In *Mein Kampf* and in his speeches Hitler talks of "extermination" (*"Vernichtung"*) and even of gassing Jews; the outcome of the First World War might well have been different, he says, if, instead of the men at the front, ten to fifteen thousand leading "Hebrews" had been exposed to poison gas. The rhetoric is deeply disturbing and deeply ominous. But did Hitler actually have a clear conception of genocide and the intent to unleash it? The problem is that he was a realist, a propagandist, and a fantasist. The realist Hitler would not have thought of genocide as a feasible proposition. In 1925 he even alluded to the tactical character of his antisemitism. It was politically expedient to "select but one enemy that everyone can recognize: he is the only guilty one. . . . And this enemy is the Jews."[4] The gangster and self-publicist Hitler would undoubtedly have relished the threatening sound of murder. Would the obsessive antisemite Hitler have seriously entertained the fantasy of genocide? Looking back in 1941 and again at the end of the war, Hitler claimed that he had followed a straight path to genocide.[5] Yet on other occasions he acknowledged that *Mein Kampf* was no blueprint.[6]

How literally then should we take his rhetoric of extermination? After all, the word *Vernichtung* (which can mean destruction, eradication, as well as extermination) was part of the wider political vocabulary applied in situations in which the physical extinction of a group or a people was inconceivable. To take one example, a National Liberal speech in 1907 included the passage "For us National Liberals there is one clear political task: a fight to the finish [*Vernichtung*] against the 'center.'"[7] The extensive parasitological metaphors have also to be seen in the context of an established radical discourse on the dangers of the Jewish presence. The German ideologist Paul de Lagarde, writing before the turn of the century, was already talking about the elimination of bacilli.[8] Some historians have argued that there is therefore a continuity of intent stretching from nineteenth-century antisemitic theorists such as Wilhelm Marr, Eugen Dühring, and de Lagarde through to the Holocaust,[9] but it seems extremely unlikely that Hitler's precursors really conceived of the mass biological destruction of hundreds of thousands or millions of individuals.

True, unlike Marr or Dühring Hitler wrote *after* the First World War, an experience that rendered conceivable the idea of millions dying through the modern technology of death. But his comments about gassing at the front were more a strategy of blackmail than a prefiguration of genocide. A crucial assumption in Hitler's mental universe was that the Jews—an international force—had been in league with the enemy. Thus, holding them hostage in wartime might be particularly effective, and gassing a few thousand would keep the rest quiescent. This proposal is lethal enough, but it does not suggest that the gas chambers of the 1940s were being imagined in the 1920s. In other words, there is no straight line from Hitler's rhetoric of extermination to the genocidal plans of Wannsee. What we can say is that Hitler's rhetoric was murderously ambiguous. At its core was his commitment to getting the Jews out of Germany. "The final aim," Hitler wrote as early as 1919, "must be the uncompromising removal of the Jews altogether."[10] Surrounding the core was an ultimately catastrophic combination of gangsterish threats and murderous flights of fantasy.

EMIGRATION AND AMBIGUITY

The same murderous ambiguity is evident when we switch our search for Wannsee's antecedents from the ideology of the 1920s to the policy of the 1930s. The ferocious antisemitism is obvious. From the moment Hitler acceded to power on January 30, 1933, Germany's Jews found themselves on the firing line. Continuing a pattern all too familiar in the months before Hitler was appointed chancellor, Nazi stormtroopers and Hitler Youth members embarked on kicking and window-smashing sprees against Jewish targets. Within a few weeks, the regional gauleiters had taken up the campaign, fomenting organized attacks against Jewish businesses in one district after another.[11] A national, government-sponsored boycott of Jewish businesses at the beginning of April was followed by a purge of the civil service. Between 1933 and 1934 Jews were removed almost completely from German public life. After a brief lull, and with a further interruption during the period around the Berlin Olympic Games, the period 1935–37 saw a whole raft of further measures: Jews lost their citizenship, were forbidden to have sexual relations with Aryans, and were denied access to almost every public amenity.[12] Toward the end of 1937, the intensity of the assault was ratcheted up several more notches. Jews were denied virtually any possibility of earning an independent living. The regime massively increased the pressure to emigrate. On *Kristallnacht,* November 9, 1938, Nazi thugs smashed through the doors and windows of almost every remaining Jewish home and business in the country. By the outbreak of the Second World War, persecution in Germany had progressed to an astonishing degree; the country's remaining Jews were a huddled, terrified remnant, living off savings and communal charity.

Yet the tide of discriminatory measures that engulfed the Jewish community with such breathtaking speed was sweeping toward the goal of a Jew-free society, not murder. After the *Anschluss* with Austria in 1938, special centers were established in Vienna and later in Berlin to "facilitate" Jewish emigration. The aim was not even vaguely to hold Jews in readiness for later disposal—on the contrary, the farther they were from Germany's reach the better. As late as April 1940, the hardliners in the Reich Security Main Office (RSHA) ordered that Jewish emigration be pursued with increased emphasis.[13] The energy expended makes no sense if policy even secretly was aiming at murder. The Nazis' principal goals up to the war were to remove Jewish influence, remove Jewish wealth, and remove the Jews from Germany. The road to Wannsee was to be twisted indeed.[14]

More worrying than either the overt or the covert goals behind anti-Jewish measures, however, was the brutality and violence with which they were carried out. The callousness of the legal assault on the Jews was breathtaking: in a sweeping action the regime suspended most of the legal rights and safeguards contained in the Weimar constitution. Striking, too, was the readiness to deploy violence, a readiness that reached its high point on *Kristallnacht*. True, *Kristallnacht* did not represent the "norm" of Nazi Jewish policy in the 1930s; in fact, it led in some respects to a rejection of overt violence on German streets, particularly by the institutions (RSHA, SS) that were to become dominant in shaping Jewish policy thereafter. But a regime that could sanction *Kristallnacht,* it might well be argued, was capable of sanctioning anything.

HITLER AND HIS HENCHMEN

At the villa in Wannsee fifteen men, representing a variety of institutions and agencies, met to talk about murder. The relationships between them and their involvement in anti-Jewish action had been decisively formed in the 1930s. More than any specific goals laid down in that decade, it was the emerging "syndrome" of eager subordination, shared racist values, and competitive cooperation in pursuit of those values that proved the most disastrous omen for the future.

Some historians have seen in the competition between Hitler's satraps the driving force that eventually led to genocide. Antisemitic measures, so the argument runs, swept forward with neither a coherent vision nor master hand to guide them. Hitler, a late riser, slow diner, rambling speaker, and political dilettante, did not pay especially close attention to Jewish measures. Never a man to create clarity where confusion might keep his subordinates in a permanent state of insecurity, he also did not place any one person in charge of Jewish affairs. In Nazi Germany in general, the lack of clear responsibilities and the overlap between old state institutions, new party agencies, and the hybrid bodies in between encouraged competition for power. Jewish policy, therefore, provided the perfect arena for ambitious men to assert their ideological credentials. Even if he didn't focus on the details of that policy, it was known to enjoy Hitler's particular interest, and there was never going to be serious opposition: there was no Jewish "bloc" enfranchised within the system to oppose or counter any initiatives. Moreover, since the regime lacked democratic institutions to absorb grievances and demands for change, the Jewish arena was the ideal place for those ordinary party members lacking in influence to express their frustration.

In this context, Hitler has sometimes even been seen as a restraining force. "Whenever he was confronted with a choice between two courses of action," writes the historian Hans Mommsen, "he would favour the less extreme solution rather than play the part of revolutionary agitator."[15] In shaping the Nuremberg Laws, for example, Hitler did not always take the radical line. Nor, on the face of it, do the laws offer much evidence of coherent planning. Cobbled together at the last minute, it has been argued that they were an impromptu place filler conjured up when a major foreign policy statement at the end of the Nuremberg rally had to be dropped.[16] The explosion of violence on *Kristallnacht*, to take another example, has been seen as a similarly impromptu measure, and one not ordered by Hitler. Historians have pointed to the role of Goebbels in unleashing the pogrom, arguing that he was eager to regain his standing following the disgrace of a recent affair with an actress.[17]

The broad participation of different groups in making policy is indeed highly significant, as were the opportunities the fluid Nazi system offered to ambitious young men. The Wannsee Conference itself was called by a power-hungry

Heydrich, seeking to bring his counterparts into line. Yet the image of the satraps jostling for power is in need of revision. For one thing, Hitler's influence was greater than this picture suggests. No one disputes that his authority rapidly became unrivaled. He was the head of the Nazi Party and the chancellor; after 1934, he also inherited presidential powers. In addition, his massive popular acclaim and the extraordinary loyalty and devotion he enjoyed from the party's hard core put him beyond criticism or competition. True enough, Hitler was often slow to act. But the system became so attuned to his signals that a raised finger was enough. Hitler was at pains not to tie his name too closely to antisemitic measures, but even so it was he who essentially set the agenda and moved it forward. The Nuremberg Laws, for example, may have been rushed through at the end, but they were the culmination of two years in which Hitler had regularly raised the citizenship question and the Interior Ministry had given it much thought.[18] And if he did not always take the extremist position, he did not consistently play the moderate either: it was Hitler who sabotaged Interior Ministry attempts to exclude half and quarter Jews from the Nuremberg Laws.

Above all, it was Hitler who set the radical new tone in the second half of the 1930s. While pushing through economic mobilization for war, taking greater risks in foreign policy, and increasingly casting aside or demoting the conservative elites with whom he had been in partnership,

Hitler also repeatedly emphasized to party and official circles the importance of removing the Jews. "The Jews must get out of Germany," noted Goebbels after one such harangue from Hitler. "Yes, out of the whole of Europe. That will still take some time. But it will and must happen. The Führer is firmly decided upon it."[19]

Even when initiatives came from elsewhere, Hitler often exerted "downward causation." He stifled moves that he did not want or that he felt to be inopportune, while encouraging others. In February 1936, for example, the Nazi leader in Switzerland, Wilhelm Gustloff, was assassinated by a Jewish student. The Olympic Games were pending in Berlin and Hitler, recognizing the diplomatic capital to be made from restraint, forbade public protests. The fact that there were indeed none dramatically demonstrated his power.[20] Two and a half years later, when Ernst vom Rath, a secretary at the German embassy in Paris, was killed there by a Polish Jew, Herschel Grynszpan, the "spontaneous reaction" was *Kristallnacht*. Here again, recent research has shown that, contrary to historians' emphasis on Goebbels as pacemaker, Hitler himself probably gave the signal for action.[21] Göring certainly thought so. Responding to the suggestion that the perpetrators should be brought to book, Göring asked, "You want to punish Hitler?"[22]

Yet Hitler's fantasies would never have been realized without the energetic participation of others, participation that helped refine and reshape his own goals. Hitler's guidance, though decisive, was intermittent; during the war it became much more so. Raul Hilberg's list of the principal players in the Jewish question includes twenty-seven different agencies, the most important of which would be represented at Wannsee.[23] In very general terms, these agencies fell into three main groups: the party, the ministries (most of whose personnel, at least initially, were inherited from the previous regime), and the SS police empire under Heinrich Himmler.

In the early years, Jewish policy was shaped largely by interaction between party pressure, Hitler's signals, and ministerial actions. But after 1936, two new players emerged. One was Göring, whose hybrid economic empire, the Four Year Plan organization, played a major role in mobilizing the economy for war until 1942–43. In the second half of the 1930s, Göring also attained de facto leadership on the Jewish question. It was Göring also who chaired the brutal post-*Kristallnacht* meeting at which Heydrich was charged with developing a comprehensive emigration policy to clear Germany of Jews. But it was Himmler who was to be crucial in developing the Final Solution.

Himmler had originally been appointed Reich leader of the SS in January 1929, when the 280-man organization was little more than Hitler's bodyguard. By 1931, with its membership running into the thousands, the SS was given the dual function of police force and elite troop. Himmler sought to craft the SS into a racial elite, requiring its officers to show proof of "pure Aryan" descent back to 1750 and taking a personal interest in vetting their brides. After 1933, in a characteristic Nazi administrative muddle, Himmler enlarged his empire through piecemeal acquisitions first of the Bavarian and later of other regional police authorities. Only in 1936 was his position formalized. Nominally Himmler was subordinate to the Ministry of the Interior, but in reality his leadership of the SS and his close links to Hitler denied the ministry any chance of control. The Reich Security Main Office (RSHA) was created in 1939, encompassing the SS Security Service (SD) and the Security Police (the criminal police and the secret state police, or Gestapo).

As Himmler swept from leader of Hitler's bodyguard to head of the Reich security forces, his subordinate Reinhard Heydrich followed in his wake. Appointed in 1932 to head the SD, Heydrich brought the Security Police, including the Gestapo, under his wing, and in 1939 became the RSHA's first chief, reporting directly to Himmler. Until 1935, the security services devoted most of their attention to the left and the churches. But responding to Hitler's signals, in the course of 1936 Heydrich expanded the SD's Jewish section. Once he acquired control of the Gestapo, Heydrich established an analogous department there for Jews, Freemasons, and immigrants. In Heydrich's conception, the SD was to be the Reich's think tank on Jewish matters, the Gestapo its frontline combatant. When Hitler's attention to the Jews sharpened, so did the SD's interest in the question. After the

Anschluss with Austria in 1938, Heydrich created an office for Jewish emigration in Vienna to streamline the removal of Jews. But it was Göring's mandate to Heydrich after *Kristallnacht* to form a Reich Central Office for Jewish Emigration in Berlin that decisively elevated Heydrich and his staff to being leading players in the Jewish question. It was this mandate, in fact, or rather its extension in July 1941, that provided Heydrich with the formal legitimation to call the Wannsee Conference.[24]

Why did so many groups and individuals take up the war against the Jews with such enthusiasm? Historians have been understandably reluctant to believe that educated, competent bureaucrats could be driven by something as irrational as antisemitism. One unbalanced individual might harbor such an obsession, but could an entire class of educated men? Surely, their objectives would be more grounded in material interests. Certainly, in a system that placed an official ideology at the heart of its claim to rule, ideology itself became a strategic tool in the exercise and pursuit of power. Antisemitism was the badge ambitious Nazis could wear to legitimate their claims and demands. Many would have been hard put to distinguish how truly they subscribed to antisemitic beliefs and to what extent those beliefs were instruments for achieving power.

But recent research has begun to rediscover the power of antisemitism as a guiding principle, less for the German population as a whole than for an important and influential minority within German society. After all, in the early 1920s, the Nazi Party was merely one of numerous small groups advocating similar brands of ideology; far from being distinctive, the party's ethnic nationalism and virulent anti-semitism were the common currency of the radical right and continued to be so throughout the decade. Between 1930 and 1933 the party muted its public antisemitism for electoral reasons, but the ideology remained vital for internal consumption and survived in party propaganda in both overt and coded form.[25] The uprisings against Jewish businesses, organized by local Nazi Party activists as soon as the regime came to power, reflected a "sincere" and strongly felt agenda at all levels of the party.[26]

Among the conservative elite, too, there is little doubt that the goal of excluding Jews from positions of power, reducing their influence in cultural life, and limiting their numbers was widely shared. On these matters, Hitler could count on enthusiastic cooperation from significant sections of the army, the civil service, and other influential areas of society. It is striking, for example, that, even after being dismissed by the Nazis on trumped-up charges in 1938, the conservative General Fritsch could still write in a private letter that the battle against the Jews was one of the most important and most difficult tasks of National Socialism.[27] Alongside antisemitism, another point of overlap between Nazis and conservative elites was widespread toleration of violence, the result of Germany's experience of defeat in World War I and of internal civil war in the 1920s. As the historian Bernd Weisbrod shows, there was striking tacit acceptance of violence among bourgeois groups whom one might have expected to disdain it.[28] Ample evidence is provided by the public tolerance of Hitler's murderous Night of the Long Knives in 1934, a rampage of terror that killed more than a hundred people, including the former chancellor, General Schleicher, and his wife.

Highly significant, too, was the sizable minority among the educated members of the so-called war youth generation (born between 1900 and 1910 or so) who most wholeheartedly bought into the ideas of the radical right. Far more than society as a whole, the student body of the 1920s reacted to war, defeat, Germany's international humiliation, and massive economic difficulty by endorsing antisemitic and ethnic-nationalist ideas. The radical right-wing Deutscher Hochschulring won more than two-thirds of the seats in student parliaments in the early 1920s. In 1926, 77 percent of Prussian students voted to keep Jews out of the association.[29] Thus, a substantial group within this cohort was persuaded of the values of *völkisch* (that is, ethnically based) nationalism. The perceived injustice of the post-Versailles world order proved to these students the arbitrariness of international rules of law and citizenship. Indeed, the Weimar state and constitution were rejected long before Hitler came to power.[30] Hitler answered this group's desire for a new ethnic politics and for a powerful state capable of dealing with internal and external enemies.

Until 1935–36 the most obvious forms of antisemitism in the Third Reich were the vulgar, thuggish outbursts of the party, and the restrained antipathy of the conservative bureaucracy. Hitler mediated between and manipulated both strands. With the expansion of the SD and the Security Police a new kind of antisemitic grouping emerged—as fanatic and committed as the party rank and file but hostile to street violence and seeking a rational and organized solution. "If there was ever a central group responsible for the National Socialist policies of genocide and persecution," Ulrich Herbert writes, it was the three hundred or so men who made up the leadership of the security services within Heydrich's RSHA. These men would be the guiding spirits of the murderous commando and police units in occupied Europe in the early 1940s.[31]

Heydrich's staff members were extraordinarily youthful; in 1939, two-thirds of those in leadership positions were thirty-six or younger.[32] Since they were also highly educated, they exemplified the characteristics of the student cohort mentioned above. Their racist-nationalist values were all the more destructive because they were often not perceived as an ideology at all. On the contrary, many of the younger men regarded themselves as realists, inured to the flowery rhetoric of older Nazis such as Himmler, Alfred Rosenberg, or

Walter Darré.[33] They advocated a modern rational realpolitik, or, in the words of Werner Best, Heydrich's deputy, "heroic realism," in which law and the ordinary proprieties would be subordinated to the pursuit of national power.[34] It is probable that, without Hitler's leadership, antisemitism would not have figured quite so prominently in this group's concerns.[35] Even in the late 1930s, the SS newspaper *Das Schwarze Korps* was as obsessed with political Catholicism as with Jewish matters.[36] But once it responded to Hitler's agenda, this cohort, with its shared philosophy of racial struggle and its espousal of martial virtues, had the will to carry it forward.

SIGNPOSTS

The shared agenda of Hitler, party, state, and SS in the 1930s was to reduce Jewish influence and encourage Jewish emigration, not to carry out mass murder. Yet the road the Nazis traveled was littered with signposts that point more directly toward Wannsee. For one thing, the approach to emigration was contradictory.[37] Fears of a Jewish world conspiracy led the Nazis to hamper Jews' ability to emigrate, not least by restricting the destinations they might choose.[38] Above all, the progressive impoverishment of potential emigrants and the increasingly draconian export restrictions for capital and currency made it hard for Jews to leave and dissuaded other countries from accepting them.[39] Hitler repeatedly threatened that if current measures did not deal with the Jews worse would follow.[40]

In the late 1930s, Hitler began to air the idea of some kind of reservation not just for German Jews but all European Jews. In September 1938, he told the Polish ambassador Jozef Lipski he hoped to settle the Jewish question by mutual agreement with Poland, Hungary, and Romania. He was thinking of shipping the Jews to a colony. Lipski replied that if Hitler could find a solution to the problem the Poles would build a monument in his honor. In January 1939, Hitler discussed the problem at length with Eastern European leaders, indicating to the Polish minister of foreign affairs, Jozef Beck, that he favored settling the Jews in a distant land. Had the Western powers allowed him, he added, he might have chosen an African colony for the purpose.[41]

Such pronouncements reflected Hitler's belief that an international Jewish conspiracy was manipulating world events. As his foreign policy became increasingly extreme and the rest of the world correspondingly suspicious, Hitler grew more threatening toward the Jews. As early as 1931 he had warned that if war broke out, the Jews would be "crushed by the wheels of history."[42] In October 1935, the Berlin journal *Judenkenner* threatened, "If a foreign army, under orders of the Jews, should ever enter German territory then it will have to march over the corpses of slain Hebrews."[43] In the late 1930s, the warnings grew more urgent. Most notorious was Hitler's "prophecy" in a speech to the Reichstag on January 30, 1939: "if international Jewry in and outside Europe once again forced the nations into a world war the result would not be the Bolshevization of the earth and victory for the Jews but the annihilation of the Jewish race in Europe."[44]

Hitler's threats were in part a kind of blackmail. If international Jewry was manipulating world affairs, then Germany's Jews might be useful as hostages to control their brethren abroad.[45] In this sense, Hitler's comments to foreign statesmen about creating a Jewish reservation should not be taken literally. Nevertheless, his "prophecies" were not merely tactical gestures. As he saw it, the Jews were not only manipulating the world powers against Germany; they had also formed an internationalist fifth column seeking to undermine Germany from within. Germany's defeat in the First World War had been the result of their diabolical machinations. This fifth column therefore had to be removed. Beyond this specific vision of a Jewish conspiracy, Hitler's threats also showed that he saw war as offering opportunities to target more generally the racial obstacles to a "healthy" society. If postwar testimony is to be believed, Hitler promised in 1935, for example, that once war came he would institute compulsory euthanasia for the handicapped. Murders of those with mental and physical disabilities did indeed begin soon after the outbreak of hostilities.[46]

As the risk of war loomed, the rhetoric grew still more lethal. In November 1938, Himmler predicted a battle between Germans and Jews. The Jews, he warned, would be merciless if they won, unwilling to stop short of total starvation and massacre of the German people. The corollary was clear if implicit. On November 24, 1938, *Das Schwarze Korps* insisted that Jews could not continue to live in Germany. "This stage of development will impose on us the vital necessity to exterminate this Jewish sub-humanity, as we exterminate all criminals in our ordered country: by the fire and the sword! The outcome will be the final catastrophe for Jewry in Germany, its total annihilation."[47]

DEPORTATIONS TO NOWHERE

In retrospect, the outbreak of war was the decisive event in unleashing the Nazis' full murderous potential. Yet when the assault on Poland began in September 1939, Nazi thinking was still a long way from genocide.[48] Indeed, until as late as summer 1941, the regime continued to promote Jewish emigration. It would take more than two years from the start of the war before the Nazis fully embraced mass murder.

The war did, however, force a reconsideration of the Jewish question. On the one hand, the scope for Jewish emigration had been significantly reduced by the closure of British and Commonwealth territories to German refugees. On the other hand, as Poland fell into German hands the Nazis acquired a new "Jewish problem"—well over two million additional Jews under their control. What was to be done with them?

The answer emerged very rapidly, though the details shifted a little over the following weeks as radical plans for Poland were put into effect. Poland's western provinces (large parts of which had been Prussian before 1918) were to be annexed to the German Reich. Many of the Polish citizens there would be expelled to a rump Polish area under German administration, the Generalgouvernement. The eastern part of the Generalgouvernement, between the Vistula and Bug Rivers, would essentially be a "reservation" where the Jews of Poland and greater Germany could be deposited.

Despite little or no advance planning, Heydrich's staff set to work with breathtaking speed. Within three weeks of the outbreak of war, Heydrich announced that Jews could be deported into the Generalgouvernement and even into the Russian-held areas of the country.[49] Adolf Eichmann, chief of the RSHA's Jewish section, prepared for deportations involving some seventy-five thousand Jews. Yet just as striking as the speed with which the deportation program began was the swiftness of its collapse. Indeed, before the summer of 1941 only a few thousand German Jews had been dispatched to Poland from German-held territories. Even deportations of Jews from the annexed Polish territories, now the Wartheland (or Warthegau, as it was generally referred to) and West Prussia, which were supposed to be cleared of non-German inhabitants, were far more limited than planned. Indeed, there were substantially more non-Jewish Polish deportations.[50]

The matter undoubtedly took high priority. Why, then, had the Germans not achieved more? For one thing, the army had managed to ring-fence some scarce rail resources. But the main reason was a gigantic resettlement program that Himmler, now Reich commissar for the strengthening of Germandom, unfurled in 1939–40. The regime had entered into a series of agreements with foreign powers to bring "home" ethnic Germans living abroad. The regime's favored destination for these lost sheep was West Prussia and the Warthegau. Polish farmsteads in these areas were to be handed over to the immigrants, and the farmers themselves shoved over the border into the Generalgouvernement. Although thousands of Polish Jews were included in this process, all specifically Jewish resettlement or deportation from elsewhere in Germany into Poland was for the moment severely curtailed.

Resistance on the part of officials in the designated receiving areas undoubtedly slowed progress. Restive at administering a social "garbage dump," the Generalgouvernement's Governor Hans Frank aspired to create a model colony. A model colony required not the settlement but the expulsion of Jews, for prestige and racial as well as economic reasons—Frank's advisers had reported to him that the region was overpopulated. Frank thus vigorously lobbied for a stop to deportations. When Göring, concerned about the economic implications of uncontrolled population movements, sided with Frank, the idea of using Poland as a dumping ground rapidly lost momentum. On March 12, 1940, Hitler declared that the Jewish question was a matter of space and that he had none at his disposal. By November 15, 1940, therefore, only five thousand Jews from Prague, Vienna, and Mährisch-Ostrau and a thousand from Stettin had been deported.[51]

If Poland could not absorb Germany's Jews and its own were unwanted, where to go with them? The most fantastical development was the proposal of Madagascar as an alternative area of settlement. First raised in the 1930s, the idea was mooted in May 1940 by Himmler, whose interest led to an initiative by Franz Rademacher of the Foreign Office. Having made some initial investigations in the 1930s, the RSHA rushed to come up with its own plan. In June 1940, Hitler gave Admiral Erich Raeder and Mussolini to understand that he considered Madagascar a serious destination for the Jews. Eichmann's assistants studied up on the tropics and received inoculations against malaria. In Poland Hans Frank, too, took the idea very seriously, seeing it as an opportunity to empty Poland of Jews. But by August it was clear that there would be no imminent victory over Britain, whose merchant marine was needed for transporting them to Africa.[52]

As late as spring 1941, on the eve of Operation Barbarossa, the invasion of the Soviet Union, the Nazis were still committed to finding a territory to which to deport Europe's Jews.[53] Although the sense of improvisation and lack of clear planning squares with what we know of the regime, it is nevertheless astonishing that a major policy conceived in a few weeks in September and October 1939 had run aground just a few weeks later and then in effect lay dormant for eighteen months.

OCCUPIED WITH MURDER

By spring 1941, Nazi policy was incomparably closer to the territory of the Wannsee Conference than it had been in September 1939, but not because genocide had yet entered the agenda. It was rather that under the aegis of war and occupation Nazi governance and social engineering had taken an almost unimaginably brutal turn.

The concept of a Jewish reservation was very different from that of emigration (though support for emigration continued). The function of a reservation, at least as the Nazis imagined it, was to provide a punishing environment in which the Jewish race would fail to thrive. Eichmann's staff worked deliberately to select the most unhealthy areas. No one put this aspect of the program more brutally than Governor Frank: "A pleasure finally to physically assault the Jewish race. The more die, the better. . . . The Jews should notice that we have arrived. We want half or three-quarters of them east of the Vistula."[54] The switch from emigration to reservation also signaled a commitment to social engineering on a gigantic new scale. The plans on Himmler's drawing board involved truly massive population transfers that would reshape the ethnic mix of all Eastern Europe. Himmler's agenda was far from purely anti-Jewish; indeed, policy toward Jews was stymied by the wider consideration of ethnic German resettlement. But blueprints on this scale rendered conceivable what had previously been beyond imagining. And as Himmler's resettlement apparatus extended its influence into all levels of the German civilian administration in Poland, it created new pressures for action.[55]

Equally important, and here Hitler's imprint was evident, the grand design was not accompanied by commensurate careful planning. Commitments were entered into and timetables drawn up with heedless speed. Transports were dispatched hither and thither with no thought for the consequences. Even the ethnic Germans were shoved around Europe without proper calculation. By the winter of 1940–41, a quarter of a million of the returnees were still sitting in fifteen hundred reception camps waiting for resettlement. But their suffering was nothing compared with that of the hundreds of thousands of Poles and Jews uprooted from their homes and dumped in the Generalgouvernement. In a 1940 roundup of German Jews from Stettin, for example, twelve hundred people, many of them elderly, were taken at night to Poland and sent on a twenty-kilometer march along snow-covered roads. Hundreds died from their exertions. Beyond driving the victims from the train, no thought had been wasted on their fate.[56]

As well as triggering massive resettlements, war brought about another significant change. Hitler had always regarded murder as a legitimate means of political struggle. We need only look at the Night of the Long Knives in 1934, when more than one hundred of Hitler's enemies had been murdered. Occupation provided the stimulus and opportunity to deploy it much more extensively as a tool of political control and social engineering. In August 1939, Hitler decided, as Heydrich put it to his subordinates on September 7, that "the social elite in Poland" should "as far as possible be rendered harmless."[57] Heydrich established so-called *Einsatzgruppen* ("operations units"), comprising Security Police (SiPo), SD, ordinary police, and the militarized (*Waffen*) SS. These men moved in behind the Wehrmacht to deal with the enemies of the Reich. In the last third of October 1939 mass executions began, targeting, among others, teachers, academics, officers, civil servants, priests, and the mentally ill. Many Jews were among the victims—of sixteen thousand civilians killed in the six weeks following the start of the war, five thousand were Jewish, and by the end of the year probably seven thousand Jews had been killed. The operation was designed not primarily as a solution to the Jewish question but rather as a means of eliminating a potential Polish national leadership. But the habit of killing was becoming addictive.[58]

Murder was deployed as a technique of social control in a very different context as well. Just prior to the outbreak of war Hitler had authorized the creation of a special program to select and eliminate physically or mentally handicapped children who would be a burden on the state. Even before the policy began to be implemented, it was extended to include handicapped adults. Here again, the Polish and ex-Polish territories provided the research laboratory. From December 1939 on, the inmates of psychiatric hospitals were murdered in the Warthegau. Gas was used for the first time as an instrument of murder. The murder of the mentally ill provided another link in the chain that led to the killing of Jews. Sometime in spring 1940 euthanasia squads began to murder all Jews with mental health problems, not bothering with the evaluations that had been performed (albeit often arbitrarily) on earlier victims. In summer 1940, in preparation for the abortive Madagascar deportations, all mentally ill Jews in psychiatric institutions in Germany were murdered. It would still take a major psychological step to move from eliminating those Jews deemed "unworthy of life" to killing all Jews. Nevertheless, the same departments and staffs who administered the euthanasia program would later devote their energy and expertise to exterminating Jews.[59]

Beyond these examples, the Polish arena gave freer rein to the brutality and murderousness already evident in the 1930s. Again, it was Hitler who gave the all-important signals. At a meeting with army leaders on August 22, 1939, one of those present took shorthand notes of Hitler's comments: "The destruction (*Vernichtung*) of Poland is priority. The goal is the removal of the active forces and not reaching a particular line. Close your hearts to any feeling. Brutal approach."[59a] A clear indication of Hitler's central role in setting the tone can be seen in his evolving relationship with the army leadership and with ordinary soldiers. In the first weeks of the Polish occupation much of the violence against Jews came not from Heydrich's special squads (*Einsatzgruppen*) but from ordinary soldiers, whose antisemitism was aroused by the strange-looking Eastern Jews. Though the soldiers were certainly influenced by the antisemitism long promoted by the Nazis, their actions were not centrally ordered. Some officers, it is true, took part in the savage dispatching of Jews across the Polish-Soviet demarcation line. Senior army figures, however, grew increasingly concerned at such excesses and sought to curb the behavior of both their own troops and the *Einsatzgruppen.* This was the last moment when a more conventional occupation and a more restrained war might have been possible. Hitler's response was to offer amnesty to all those who had committed excesses, to withdraw the army's responsibility for the administration of Poland, and to end the military courts' jurisdiction over the SS and the *Einsatzgruppen.* Even those generals who, like Georg von Küchler, had fiercely objected to the crimes, now fell into line. Within a little more than a year and a half the army would be a docile participant in genocide.[60]

Whereas in the Reich the existing elites provided some counterweight to Nazi rule, in the East the Nazis staffed the administrations with their own. The SD and Security Police officials in particular were almost all longtime Nazis. Hostility to Poles and especially to Jews was common currency. In this climate, the pogrom-style violence of the party man, the controlled brutality of the Security Police, and the callous disregard of the "colonial" civil servant began to meld. Once the deportation program ran aground, Berlin's interest in the treatment of Jews in Poland declined, and the men at the lower level were given greater freedom to do as they would. Local measures were sufficiently diverse to disprove the existence of any coherent murder plan. But actions in Warsaw, Lublin, and elsewhere were sufficiently lethal to give rise to a widely held belief among well-informed Polish and foreign observers that once the war was over, the Jews would be eliminated altogether.[61]

STALEMATE

Within the German administration in Poland, there was no such assumption in the summer of 1940 or even in the spring of 1941. Rather there was a growing conviction that the Jews had to leave the region. As noted, Governor Frank rejected the idea of Poland as a dumping ground for them. In the course of 1939–40 a series of ideas had emerged about rational use of Polish land for the good of Germany—either under direct German settlement or as provider of resources for the Fatherland. By the summer of 1940 Frank's staff understood that the Jews and at least some of the non-Jewish Poles would have to be cleared out to make the region economically efficient. The more pressure placed on the region to provide surplus food for the Reich, the more the civilian administration sought to transfer "surplus" population farther east.[62]

Back home, frustration grew at all levels with the slow pace of Jewish expulsions. In Vienna, complaints about the continued presence of Jews could be heard from a variety of local party figures almost as soon as the war began. In December 1940 the Viennese gauleiter (regional party chief), Baldur von Schirach, added his voice to the clamor. Hitler promised support, though the subsequent expulsions were again very limited. In spring 1941, it was Goebbels's turn to complain; he, too, was told no deportations could take place at present. More than anyone, Heydrich and his subordinate Adolf Eichmann, the RSHA's official for Jewish affairs, nailed their institutional colors and prestige to the goal of clearing the Reich of Jews. When Eichmann received orders to desist after the first wave of Jewish deportations to the Generalgouvernement, for example, he insisted that one further transport be dispatched "to maintain the prestige of the state police."[63] It was a major provocation for the RSHA that every attempt to expel Jews ended in failure. Territorial solutions continued to be the official goal, but there was a mounting sense that decisive moves needed to be taken.[64] Hitler was bombarded with requests for action.

GENOCIDAL WAR BEGINS

In 1940–41, occupied Poland seethed with acts of brutality. In the little town of Izbica, the new ethnic-German mayor trained his dog to recognize the Jewish star. Women on their way to the well for water were brought down by the mayor's beloved Alsatian and murdered for sport. In Odilo Globocnik's labor camps, Jews constructing defensive fortifications along the Bug River died in droves. The guards amused themselves by making them leap from car to car on moving trains. There are thousands, even tens of thousands, of such examples, and they already convey an authentic Holocaust character. Yet at the highest level of planning genocide had still not become part of the agenda. It was the war against the Soviet Union that would make the decisive difference.

On June 22, 1941, German troops entered Soviet territory. Behind the troops swept in four motorized *Einsatzgruppen* of six hundred to a thousand men each. Karl Jäger, the head of one of the subcommandos operating within the northern group, *Einsatzgruppe* A, reported in December on the activities of his own unit:

I can now state that the aim of solving the Jewish problem for Lithuania has been achieved by Einsatzkommando 3. There are no more Jews in Lithuania apart from the work-Jews and their families. . . .

The carrying out of such actions is first and foremost a matter of organization. The decision to clear each district systematically of Jews required a thorough preparation of every single action and the investigation of the conditions in the particular district. The Jews had to be concentrated in one place or in several places. The place for the pits which were required had to be found and dug out to suit the numbers involved. The distance from the place where the Jews were concentrated to the pits was on average 4–5km. The Jews were transported to the place of execution in groups of up to 500 with gaps of at least 2km. . . .[65]

By the time of his report, mass shootings by *Einsatzkommandos* and other killing units had led to the deaths of half a million Jews. The era of genocide had begun.

This was no ordinary war, Hitler told his generals, but a fight to the death between two ideologies. The Soviet state had to be destroyed; the Communist officials were all criminals and must be treated as such.[66] The latter demand was perhaps not very different from his instruction of August 1939 that the Polish leadership be eliminated. The disastrous difference as far as Jews were concerned was that Hitler believed they were at the heart of the Communist system.

Hitler's aim was the elimination of the "Judeo-Bolshevik intelligentsia." In Russia, therefore, the campaign against the elites was to be from the beginning also a campaign against the Jews, with the limits of Jewish culpability and participation poorly defined.

Hitler could count on the enthusiastic endorsement of the Security Police and SD. The tasks of the four *Einsatzgruppen* sent into the Soviet Union had been planned by Reinhard Heydrich in the months before Barbarossa. The same highly educated elite in the higher echelons of the SD now provided the cool commanders of the *Einsatz* squads. The detailed head counts sent back to Berlin, listing carefully and separately the Jewish men, women, and children shot during the reporting period, reveal for the first time in its full horror the unique fusion of annihilatory ideology and bureaucratic fastidiousness that characterized Heydrich's staff. Striking, too, was the degree to which the army now accepted anti-Jewish measures as essential to the fight against the Soviet leadership. Sharing Hitler's anti-Bolshevism and antisemitism and having learned subservience in Poland, the army high command willingly plotted a new kind of war.[67] They accepted the infamous *Kommissarbefehl* (commissar order) of June 6, which ordered that all political commissars attached to the Red Army be shot.[68] They further agreed that Himmler's men would have "special tasks" within their zone of operation, and that they were entitled to act against the civilian population on Himmler's authority. For both the army and the *Einsatzkommandos,* anti-Bolshevism and antipartisan actions became the legitimation for action against Jewish civilians.[69]

The Soviet war was predicated on murder in another sense, too. As a number of historians have emphasized recently, Hitler's all or nothing military strategy, and indeed his longer-term settlement plans, depended on the ruthless commandeering of Soviet resources, above all its foodstuffs.[70] On May 2, 1941, a meeting between military and civilian economic experts concluded that war could be sustained beyond the end of the year only if German soldiers on Russian soil were fed from Russian supplies. Their dry assessment was that "doubtless tens of millions [*Zigmillionen*] of people will starve to death."[71] The German high command deliberately made no provision for feeding the expected millions of Soviet prisoners. The result was an astonishingly high death toll among the POWs—initially far higher than the number of Jews who were killed. Over the summer, as pressures on food resources grew—because the army failed to advance sufficiently and because farmers, caught in the war, had not planted their fields—there was increasing talk of eliminating "useless eaters."[72] In September the rations for POWs were lowered still further, and by the end of 1941 a staggering *two million* Soviet prisoners had died in German hands.[73] This deliberate failure to plan for appropriate supplies shows that millions of deaths off the battlefield were a calculated and integral part of the campaign.

Barbarossa, then, created murderous imperatives and altered the whole tone of war. But does this mean that there was from the beginning a clear decision to murder all Soviet Jews or that a more limited strategic concept (eliminating the Judeo-Bolshevik intelligentsia) later widened into something more comprehensive? Unfortunately, much of Heydrich's planning is concealed from us. We know far less about the instructions given to the *Einsatzgruppen* commanders than we do about the Wehrmacht's basic directives. All that has been preserved is a précis of Heydrich's instructions handed on in June to the Higher SS and Police Leaders (HSSPF) in the Soviet Union.[74] This document indicates that "all Jews in the service of Party and state" should be targeted, an instruction not intrinsically genocidal though vague in the extreme. It seems quite possible that Heydrich's verbal instructions to the *Einsatzgruppen* went beyond the written orders.[75]

If we look at the actual practice of the killing squads, we see that they began by targeting a narrower group of state officials and Jews in leading positions but very rapidly began to include all Jewish men of military age.[76] A few weeks later, in July to August, women and children began to be included, and in August to September squads moved to eliminate entire communities.[77] Was this the stepwise implementation of a preexisting plan or did the instructions change over the summer? If they did, who ordered the more extensive killing? Postwar trial testimony of captured *Einsatzgruppen* and -*kommando* leaders is extremely contradictory, as are the progress reports they submitted during the war.[78] While confirming the general trend toward greater comprehensiveness, the reports also indicate considerable variations in local commanders' interpretations of their brief. As early as July 1941, the leader of *Einsatzgruppe* A believed that the special conditions in the Soviet Union made possible the murder of all Jews.[79] Yet even in September, *Einsatzgruppe* C did not seem to think that eliminating Jews was its principal task.[80]

Whatever instructions the group and local commanders had initially received, therefore, had been susceptible to narrower or broader interpretation. This suggests that the initial orders were not clearly genocidal but that their definition of the Jewish elite was so loose that it enabled something quite close to genocide—namely, the elimination of all Jewish men of working age. Once killings on that scale had been carried out, it often seemed but a small step to widen the scope of murder. The widows and children of the murdered men did not look like an economically viable community, particularly in view of the intensifying food shortages.

Hitler certainly established the general climate for this radicalization of policy. We know that he asked for regular reports on *Einsatzgruppen* activities, and a shooting may even have been filmed for him.[81] Moreover, at an important meeting on July 16, after which he gave Alfred Rosenberg, minister for the occupied eastern territories, jurisdiction over those areas no longer directly under military command, Hitler announced that Germany would never relinquish the conquered Soviet territories. All measures necessary for a final settlement—such as shooting and deportation—should be taken. Stalin's partisan war provided the excuse to "exterminate anything opposing us"—"anyone who even looks at us the wrong way should be shot."[82] Hitler made these statements in confident anticipation of a rapid victory. Toward the end of July, however, it became apparent that progress was slower than expected and that supplying the troops had become a major problem. Now it was Göring's turn to send some harsh signals down. On July 27–28, he ordered that all food production in the occupied eastern territories be centrally controlled and allocated only to those who worked for Germany. Some sections of the German civilian administration in occupied Soviet territory had already begun to distinguish between Jews and non-Jews; Göring now extended this discrimination to the whole of the occupied Soviet Union.[83]

It was above all Himmler who conveyed the need for more radical measures. On July 17, 1941, Hitler made him responsible for security in the civilian regions in the East now under Rosenberg's jurisdiction. From July 15 to 20, Himmler was in the Führer's headquarters. We do not know what communications he had with Hitler, but whatever took place, Himmler rapidly moved from policies that still might be characterized as murderous security measures to ones that could only be seen as genocidal—solving the "Jewish problem" in large areas of the conquered Soviet Union by killing. Himmler's actions reflected not only his security mandate from Hitler but also his informal (later official) quest to extend his role as Reich commissar for the strengthening of Germandom from Poland to the former Soviet territories. Within a week of his appointment, Himmler quadrupled the number of SS men operating behind army lines. He also assigned the police reserve battalions to his direct subordinates in the field, the Higher SS and Police Leaders (HSSPF). Through the HSSPF, Himmler began to press for the radical cleansing of huge swaths of territory for both security and settlement purposes. At the end of July there may still have been a little hesitation at ordering the killings of women and children—for example, in an operation to drive them into the Pripet Marshes—but only a little.[84] Increasingly, the HSSPF took the leading role in the killing process, and the SS brigades and police battalions under their direction eventually murdered far more Jews than the original *Einsatzgruppen*.[85]

Overall, the evidence does not support the idea that there was one single clear-cut order to murder all Jews. The point in time at which the individual *Einsatzgruppen* widened the scope of their killing varied considerably. What we can say is that in the murderous climate fostered by Hitler, a variety of agencies, with the Himmler-Heydrich axis at the center, worked together to push measures forward. The *Einsatzgruppen* leaders, most of them drawn from the educated, ideologically homogeneous upper ranks of the Security Police and SD, interpreted their brief liberally. In the latter half of July and first half of August, Himmler, perhaps under instructions from Hitler, moved toward a more openly genocidal line. As economic pressures increased, the SS–Security Police leadership found further support for their actions from civilian officials who complained about undesirable elements making claims on scarce resources. The civilian administration in Lithuania and some field commanders in the Wehrmacht drew up agreements with the SS to get rid of the useless eaters left alive after the first shootings. By August 1941 at the latest, the fate of Soviet Jewry was sealed.[86]

3

MASS MURDER TO GENOCIDE

The weeks following the outbreak of war against the Soviet Union had changed the climate irrevocably. Assumptions about what was feasible were reformulated, inhibitions about what was intolerable were progressively discarded. As early as July, Himmler's thoughts turned to gas as an alternative to shooting. At the same time, knowledge of the shootings spread among Nazi elites in Germany and elsewhere in occupied Europe, and their perception of what was possible also began to change. A psychological threshold was irrevocably crossed.

Yet widespread murder in the lawless conditions behind the military front line was still significantly different from the systematic killing of Jews all across Europe, the project expressed in the Wannsee Protocol. How and when was this transition effected? Unfortunately, our need for precise answers is greater than the ability of the documentation to supply them. Despite the absence of evidence, most historians continue to assume that, however twisted the road may have been, Hitler must at some point have made the ultimate decision to murder European Jewry. His role in redefining the character of warfare and introducing pacification through murder and social engineering had been crucial. But how closely did he now direct the killing of Jews? Was his approval given or merely presumed? Did the transition from mass killing to genocide involve a clear decision, or was the program outlined at Wannsee more of a retrospective codification of a process already under way?

Even more than in peacetime, Hitler carefully concealed his involvement in the Jewish question.[1] The paucity of official records is not compensated by the existence of private ones. Hitler kept no diary and sent no letters expressing views on the Jewish question. A number of those close to him recorded his views, but often their notes are ambiguous too. The challenge, therefore, is to ascertain not only what Hitler's subordinates *thought* he said but also whether they got it right. In any case, we have virtually no record of probably the most important channel of communication on the Jewish question, Hitler's conversations with Himmler. The occasional pertinent entries in Himmler's appointment diary are abbreviated and cryptic.

Those statements of Hitler's that we do have are of course forthright enough. But Hitler's rhetoric, as we have seen, is

deliberately inflammatory. There is a relationship between
his brutal words and his brutal policies but it is not a direct
one. Take Hitler's "prophecy" of January 1939 that a future
world war would lead to the extermination of Jews in
Europe. There is no doubt his warning was significant, not
least in setting the rhetorical pitch for his subordinates. For
some historians, it represents a clear threat of genocide. Yet
there is no evidence that mass extermination was being
planned in 1939, and Hitler himself made little reference to
the prophecy throughout the whole of 1940. It's impossible
to tell, then, whether his statements demonstrate clear
intent or even to ascertain precisely what the intent might
have been. Hitler warned that annihilation would follow if
the Jews were to plunge Europe into *world* war. Is it possible
that he did not yet see the conflict with Britain and the
Commonwealth as world war? Something that might support such an idea is that in January 1941, when war with the
Soviet Union was in the offing, Hitler recalled his prophecy
of two years earlier and thereafter returned to it more often.
Yet his timing then may have been a response to other
developments that were changing his thinking rather than
evidence of consistent understanding of what "world war"
meant.

It is also uncertain whether the "annihilation" of Jews in
Europe implied a clearly formulated desire for their death or
simply for their complete banishment. Hitler repeatedly
talked of the need to drive the Jews out of Germany by force.

Brutal means were required to cleanse the racial state. But his pronouncements seldom unequivocally crossed the line from physical removal to physical extermination.

Altogether, Hitler's table talk sounds not like the clear goal setting of a policy maker but like the late-night ramblings of a know-nothing at a *Bierkeller.* The thought that this speaker was presiding over the fate of millions is almost inconceivable. With monologues as disjointed as these, how could even his closest confidants know his intentions? Were the issue not genocide, of course, Hitler's responsibility would be beyond question. We would not be interrogating his language so scrupulously. We would accept almost any of his statements as proof of his intentions. But the Holocaust is so monstrously innovative that we are obliged to understand precisely how the taboos could be broken.

EXTENDING MURDER: JULY 1941

Until recently, most historians would have chosen one of two moments as the most likely point at which Hitler committed himself to eliminating European Jewry. One occurred sometime in mid-July, just before Himmler moved to extend the killings in the Soviet Union, the other in mid-September, when Hitler approved the deportation of German Jews eastward.

In mid-July, as we have seen, Hitler, anticipating imminent victory over the Soviet Union, made some fundamental

policy decisions, laying down harsh guidelines for the "pacification" and colonization of Soviet territory. It was in the
wake of these decisions that Himmler radically widened the
scope of the killings in the Soviet Union. Goebbels wrote in
his diary at the beginning of August that "the Führer is
convinced that his former prophecy in the Reichstag is
being confirmed: if Jewry succeeded once more in provoking
a world war, it would end with the annihilation of the Jews.
It is being confirmed in these weeks and months with a cer-
tainty that seems almost uncanny."[2] The commandant of
Auschwitz, Rudolf Höss, stated after the war that he was
summoned by Himmler in the summer of 1941 and told
that Auschwitz, then an "ordinary" concentration camp, was
going to be an extermination center for the Jews. On trial in
Jerusalem, Adolf Eichmann, too, said he learned that summer about a fundamental Hitler decision. It was around this
time that Himmler began thinking of using gas as an alternative to shooting.[3] Friedrich Suhr, a legal expert in the
RSHA, was given an official title: "Official for the Final
Solution of the European Jewish Question, Particularly
Abroad." On July 28, 1941, Viktor Brack, the man in charge
of T4, the so-called euthanasia operation, asked for support
from the military economic administration for a major forthcoming action, yet as far as we know, no such action was
planned within the euthanasia program.

Most significant, there is Göring's infamous *Ermächtigung*

(authorization) to Heydrich of July 31, 1941, which many historians see as the authentic inception of genocide:[4]

> In completion of the task entrusted to you in the edict dated January 24, 1939, of solving the Jewish question by means of migration or evacuation in the most convenient way possible, given the present conditions, I herewith charge you with making all necessary preparations with regard to organizational, practical, and financial aspects for an overall solution of the Jewish question in the German sphere of influence in Europe.
>
> Insofar as the competencies of other central organizations are affected, these should be involved.
>
> I further charge you with submitting to me promptly an overall plan of the preliminary organizational, practical, and financial measures for the execution of the intended final solution of the Jewish question.

Thanks to recent research in the former Soviet archives we now know a little more about the background to the Göring document. Heydrich himself produced the first draft in March 1941, noting at the time that he had submitted it to Göring for signature but that agreement with Rosenberg was required before it could be authorized.[5] Rosenberg was the minister designate for the occupied Soviet territories, and it would seem that Heydrich was seeking Göring's approval to develop a new deportation policy into Siberia or

some eastern Soviet territory, now that the Polish deportations had failed.[6] Discussions clarified Rosenberg's attitude
and involvement, enabling Heydrich to re-present the draft
in July.[7] Of course, the terms in the authorization—"overall
solution" (*Gesamtlösung*) and "final solution" (*Endlösung*) of
the Jewish question—would soon be euphemisms for murder. By the end of November, when Heydrich attached this
document to the invitations to the Wannsee Conference as
proof of his authority, there is little doubt that "final solution" had lost any other meaning. But up to 1941, Heydrich,
for one, regularly distinguished between "interim" and "final"
solutions without meaning genocide in the latter case—for
example, in relation to the future of the Protectorate.[8] We do
not need to assume that the terms had attained their clear
code meaning by July.

On closer inspection, the other evidence for a July decision for genocide also looks problematic. Both Höss's and
Eichmann's testimonies lack credibility. Höss's meeting
with Himmler almost certainly took place at least nine
months later than he remembered.[9] Above all, Höss made
clear that at the point when he learned about Auschwitz's
new function, other extermination camps in Poland were
already functioning—and that can only have been in 1942.[10]
Eichmann, for his part, was at pains to establish a clear set of
orders that absolved him of responsibility. In the interviews
he gave in Argentina and in his first interrogation, he said
that he learned about the Final Solution only at the end of

1941. But later he claimed to remember hearing of Hitler's order in the summer of that year. However, the details he attached to the memory, relating to a visit to the Belzec camp, meant that he could not have heard before November 1941.[11]

What we find in spring and summer 1941, in fact, is growing clamor from different groups hoping to use the Soviet territory as a dumping ground for German and other European Jews. Hitler himself made various pronouncements about the deportation of Europe's Jews. Before the start of the Russian campaign he had promised Hans Frank that the Jews would be removed from the Generalgouvernement in the foreseeable future.[12] On July 22, he announced to Croatian Marshal Slavko Kvaternik his intention to deport Jews, saying it was a matter of indifference to him whether they were sent to Madagascar or to Siberia.[13] Whether his talk of deportation was sincere or not, other Nazi officials certainly concluded from conversations with Hitler that European Jews were going to be sent to the East. Having failed in March 1941 to send Jews to the Polish Generalgouvernement, Goebbels noted delightedly in June that they were all looking forward to expelling their Jews. For Hans Frank, the governor of the Generalgouvernement, Russia represented the answer to his prayers.[14]

Doubts must remain. Did the Germans really intend to deport Jews to the Soviet Union when, even if Germany won the war, border skirmishes were certain to continue for some time? Were they likely to deposit their archenemy, the Jews, in an area where the Jews could make contact with Germany's other enemies? Possibly—if the borders were suitably policed.[15] What is certain is that the deportation plans had a new and consciously genocidal aspect. None of those seeking to drive Jews to the Pripet Marshes or to Siberia would have expected or hoped the deportees would thrive. As news of the events in the Soviet Union spread among the Nazi elite—and we know that in the course of the summer knowledge of what was happening to the Jews there became quite widespread—so the sense of what deportation to the Soviet Union meant must have changed too. When in August, for example, Nazi officials in France put forward the idea of deporting Europe's Jews to Russia, they were proposing not the separate existence of a Jewish people but its disappearance in hostile terrain. The acceptability of killing was spreading out from the Soviet Union, an invitation to key Nazis all across Europe.[16]

DEATH AND DEPORTATION: SEPTEMBER 1941

In March 1941, Hitler had resisted initiatives by Heydrich and Goebbels to dispatch Jews to Poland. In July 1941, he rejected attempts by Governor Frank to claim the Pripet Marshes from the occupied Soviet territory and use them as a Jewish reservation. In August, he blocked a new deportation plan of Heydrich's. The war needed to be won before major deportations could be resumed.

A variety of figures continued to urge not only deportations but also other special measures—above all forcing German Jews to wear a special star, as had long been required of Jews in Poland and was now being required in the Czech Protectorate. Goebbels, keen to liberate Berlin of its sizable Jewish presence, visited Hitler on August 18. Hitler agreed that German Jews should wear the yellow star—a considerable step and tacit recognition that voluntary emigration was no longer the anticipated fate of most German Jews. The star would make them easy to round up. Hitler promised, too, that Jews would be deported before the end of the war. But he still resisted any immediate action; the trains could be dispatched only after the eastern campaign was over.[17]

Sometime in mid-September 1941, however, Hitler changed his mind. After meeting Otto Abetz, the German ambassador to France, who requested that all Jews be deported from occupied France, and hearing from the gauleiter of Hamburg, Karl Kaufmann, who requested that Jewish housing be made available to German victims of the recent British bombing raids, Hitler now said that German Jews and those from the Czech Protectorate could be deported immediately.[18] Other European Jews were also targeted: in the same month, the deportation of French Jews, initially limited to those in detention, was also announced.[19]

In contrast to the onset of Operation Barbarossa, where

we can see an obvious stimulus to new actions, Hitler's reversal of his line on deportations seems less clearly motivated. The immediate trigger to act against Jews may have been the Soviets' sudden deportation of Volga Germans to Siberia on September 13–15.[20] Hitler was a vengeful man and Goebbels's diary entry of September 9 (after Stalin's decision to deport the Volga Germans had been announced) makes evident that the regime regarded Stalin's announcement as legitimation to take more radical steps.[21] For Hitler, it will have been a fitting part of his revenge to start the deportations of Jews in October, at exactly the point when the Soviets were to have been defeated in the Nazis' original plans. He may have been helped to his decision by Rosenberg, now minister for the eastern territories, who had concluded—no doubt on the basis of the Germans' own deportations—that most of the ethnic Germans would not survive those initiated by the Soviets. It was Rosenberg who on September 14 had passed on via his liaison officer at the army high command, Otto Bräutigam, the idea of deporting the Jews from Central Europe to the East as a "reprisal" to the Soviet action.[22]

At the very least, Hitler's decision on deportation was a significant radicalization of existing measures and moved him significantly closer to realizing his long-expressed desire to rid Europe of its Jews. But where were the Jews to go? Poland was no better equipped to take on the Jews than it had been in August. The Soviet campaign was not over.

Hitler had given the green light for deportations under conditions no more favorable than those earlier, when he had blocked them. For some historians, this is crucial evidence that Hitler had now either already decided on genocide or was on the brink of that decision.[23]

Other developments reinforce the idea that September 1941 was the decisive turning point. The policy of mass shootings began to be extended beyond the borders of the Soviet Union into Serbia and Galicia. Experiments in gassing Jews took place in Mogilev and Minsk between September 3 and 18. In the Warthegau, the machinery of murder began to be put in place from October. In November, mobile gas vans were utilized in the Warthegau to murder Jews in the Kalisch district, while preparations at the Chelmno camp site date from the beginning of October. Farther west, within the Generalgouvernement, too, there were moves toward creating at least one gas camp. And sometime in the autumn the first experiments were carried out with cyanide at Auschwitz, though to kill Soviet POWs.[24]

Hitler's command for deportation did not tie in with these various initiatives very neatly. Logically, if mass murder was already on the agenda, it would have made more sense to hold the Jews in Germany until the camps were ready.[25] Moreover, Hitler seemed very uncertain over the following weeks as to whether the timing for deportations was opportune. His hesitation adds credence to the view that, in a rage at Soviet deportations of Volga Germans, Hitler had given in to pressure without having formulated a new master plan. There is also evidence that Hitler still held to the belief that until the United States entered the war the Jews were useful as hostages. Four days after Hitler agreed to the deportations, Werner Koeppen, Rosenberg's personal aide, noted that the Führer had not yet made a decision about reprisals against German Jews; Koeppen had heard that Hitler would act if the United States entered the war.[26]

Thus when Hitler and Himmler agreed in September that, as a temporary step, sixty thousand Jews should be deported not to the Generalgouvernement but to the Lodz ghetto in the Warthegau, it seems that what they had in mind was deportation, not murder. As Himmler wrote to Arthur Greiser, gauleiter of the Warthegau, on September 18, the plan was to deport Jews first to temporary quarters in the Lodz ghetto, then, in the spring, farther east.[27] (In late September Hitler was again so confident about the military situation in the Soviet Union that this timetable may have seemed realistic.)[28] After protests from Lodz, however, the figure was reduced to twenty-five thousand Jews and Gypsies. In early October, when Hitler called for the entire Czech Protectorate to be cleared, he suggested that the Czech Jews should not first be sent to Poland but should immediately be directed farther east, that is, to the Soviet Union. Although it is unknown whether Hitler expected the deportees to be murdered on Soviet soil, it seems clear, at the very least, that he had not yet arrived at a plan for exterminating the Jews on Polish territory.[29]

THE MIDDLE MANAGERS OF MURDER

Over the last decade or so, our understanding of the events of these months has been transformed by a series of studies drawing on previously inaccessible German material held in Soviet bloc archives. These studies have shown that while regional leaders may have responded to common signals and pressures, their various initiatives in these months were probably not part of a central plan.

Starting in the summer of 1941 the notion spread that it was acceptable, even appropriate, to shoot Jews. Within the Soviet Union, all sorts of local units—including regular units of the German army—decided on their own to extend their killing operations.[30] Outside the Soviet Union, in Serbia, the newly arrived commander, General Franz Böhme, introduced a radical new policy of reprisal against partisan attacks: all Jewish men of arms-bearing age were placed in a "reservoir" of potential hostages and a hundred were shot for every German soldier killed. Böhme made no distinction between Jews or different patterns of behavior. The official explanation was that the Jews were linked to the partisan war, but it was clear that this was not the case. Even Jews who had been deported to Serbia from Austria, Bohemia, and

Danzig before the beginning of the partisan uprisings and who had no conceivable part in them were included. Böhme referred to the killings as shooting hostages. But if these were "hostages," they were so only in the abstract sense that the Germans were holding the conspiratorial force "World Jewry" ransom.[31]

The ratio of a hundred Jews for every German was not Böhme's own idea; it had been dictated from on high. Moreover, soon after his arrival in Serbia in September he had been approached by German officials urging a speedy resolution to the Jewish question. The officials, it seems, had been thinking of deportation. But though he undoubtedly responded to such signals, Böhme had no central instructions to make Jews his principal target. Instead, the historian Walter Manoschek has concluded, by the autumn of 1941 no special orders were necessary for such genocidal policy decisions to be made. Whatever their disagreements on other questions, when it came to the Jews, all the German authorities cooperated. What's more, the willingness to kill was not the result of special indoctrination, such as that given to SS men. It was the regular army that carried out most of the murders. By the end of the year, there were virtually no adult Jewish males left in Serbia. Following the murder of the women and children in early 1942, Serbia became one of the first countries to be "Jew free."[32]

Eastern Galicia offers a similar picture of regional initiative, drawing on the "lessons in shooting" provided by the Soviet experience. On October 12, the security forces embarked on a huge killing program, eliminating thousands of Jewish men, women, and children in the first two weeks, tens of thousands in the next couple of months.[33] Although Himmler had held meetings with regional officials in early September and some postwar testimony intimates that a killing order was passed down the line, the report submitted in 1942 by the principal instigator of murders in the region, the Galician district SS and police leader (SSPF) Fritz Katzmann, does not support this contention. Himmler's direct orders to kill are clearly confirmed only much later—in July and October 1942 and May and October 1943. Of course, the Galician officials undoubtedly knew that Himmler and, above him, Hitler were willing to endorse mass murder. But the shootings seem to have been a regional initiative designed in the short term to thin out the population so that "manageable" ghettos could be created. Regional officials like Katzmann, it seems, were also thinking of the possibility of total eradication of the Jews through murder.[34]

Killings in the Soviet Union had other repercussions, too. Relatively early on Himmler concluded that some other form of murder might be preferable to shooting. The search for alternative methods probably began in July 1941—there is a cryptic memo from Himmler about gas installations, and there is other evidence, too, that plans were already afoot to gas Jews either on Soviet soil or in Eastern Europe.[35] Postwar testimony suggests that Himmler was so badly affected by witnessing a shooting in August that he commissioned Arthur Nebe (or perhaps the HSSPF in central Russia, Erich von dem Bach-Zelewksi, who in turn commissioned Nebe) to develop alternatives, so as to avoid the spiritual burdening of his men. Nebe, as well as being the head of *Einsatzgruppe* B, was in charge of the institute involved in developing mobile gas vans to kill mentally ill patients in Poland.

Perhaps in response to Himmler's concerns, perhaps independently, various local officials in the annexed Polish territories also began to wonder about other ways of getting rid of the Jews. A notorious memorandum sent to Eichmann on July 16 by the head of the SD in Posen, Rolf Heinz Höppner, summarized discussions under way among the advisers to Gauleiter Arthur Greiser. A series of proposals had been made for dealing with the Jewish problem: those who could work should be put in forced labor columns; women of childbearing age should be sterilized, so that with this generation the problem would be solved. In winter, however, there would not be enough food to feed all the Jews. "It should be seriously considered if the most humane solution would not be to kill those Jews not capable of work with some quick acting means. This would certainly be more pleasant than allowing them to starve to death," Höppner wrote. "The things sound in part fantastical," he added, "but in my view they are thoroughly practicable."[36]

On September 3, Höppner sent another memorandum, thirteen pages long, proposing that the organizations in the annexed territories that handled deportations to the Generalgouvernement be expanded into a body responsible for deportations from a much wider area—that is, the whole Reich. He understood that certain fundamental decisions had not yet been made. Nor did he know the intentions of top officials. He imagined nevertheless that the Soviet territory would provide adequate space. But the important thing, as he saw it, was to know the Jews' final fate, and here he asked a question: Was the goal to guarantee them permanently the promise of life or was it to exterminate them completely?[37]

This memorandum shows that there was still uncertainty but also that the unthinkable was now being thought, at least in the Warthegau. What is not clear is to what extent Höppner was picking up signals from on high. Whatever the case, Höppner was clearly responding to a growing sense in both the Warthegau (particularly with respect to Lodz) and the Generalgouvernement that in the absence of a program of immediate deportation the problems of food and epidemic raised by the Jewish population required drastic action.

In the late summer and early autumn two new factors influenced policy in the annexed territories and the Generalgouvernement. The first was Hitler's September decision to allow the deportation trains to run once more. Whatever Hitler's immediate intentions, the eastward deportation of German Jews created yet more pressures and challenges for the receiving territories. Until then, the lack of capacity (above all in the Generalgouvernement) had repeatedly sty-mied the deportation aspirations of Heydrich and Eichmann. Now, the deportations were not to be blocked, and the receiving authorities had to deal with the problem as best as they could. Despite fierce protest from the mayor of Lodz, from Commissar Wilhelm Kube in Minsk, and from author-ities in Latvia and Lithuania, the deportation trains started rolling.

Construction of the Chelmno gas camp began within two weeks of Himmler's decision that the first deportations would be sent to Lodz, an already overcrowded ghetto. Look-ing back on events in a May 1942 letter to Himmler, Greiser indicated that the killing of a hundred thousand Polish Jews from the region was specifically authorized by Himmler, through Heydrich, as a quid pro quo for the willingness of the Warthegau authorities to receive deportees from Ger-many. While authorization for the killings came from the top, the initiative had come from the locality, and the goal was the solution of a regional "problem" rather than the implementation of a more comprehensive program.[38]

The second major development affected the Generalgou-vernement, which unlike the annexed former Polish territory in the Warthegau was not directly affected by Hitler's depor-tation decision. Here, the biggest impact of the Soviet cam-paign was to disappoint earlier expectations of offloading the region's Jews. Over the course of 1941, the whole of the administration, from Hans Frank down, had been anticipating the Jews' rapid removal into the territory of the former Soviet Union. But in mid-October Frank learned that the slow progress of the war meant there was little prospect of such removals. The dragging Soviet campaign also had economic implications for his region. The failure to gain control of Soviet resources exacerbated the already severe food crisis in the Generalgouvernement—and on top of everything else there was a very poor harvest in 1941. Pressure grew for the removal of "useless mouths."[39] For Frank's staff the Jews represented a constant source of illegal activity. Not surprising given that the restrictions imposed on Polish Jews denied them any legal opportunity to earn enough even just to survive. A fatal two-pronged development ensued. The hardline radicals in Himmler's almost autonomous police empire in Poland undertook increasingly violent measures, while the civilian administration imposed exclusionary and persecutory measures on the Jewish population that made killing seem the only option.[40]

The Lublin district SS and police leader Odilo Globocnik had shown ruthless energy in developing murderous labor projects for Jews in the Bug region. In 1941 he unfolded far-reaching plans to Germanize Lublin, expelling all Poles and Jews from the area. On July 20, 1941, Himmler commissioned him to prepare the ground for German settlement of the Lublin district and then farther east. At the beginning of October, Globocnik urgently sought a meeting with Himmler to discuss proposals for clearing the Lublin area of its

Jews. Globocnik's letter of October 1 suggests that up till then he had heard nothing of a comprehensive program of murder. His meeting with Himmler took place on October 13, the same day that Governor Frank discovered that no deportations were likely to take place in the near future. The outcome of Globocnik's consultation with Himmler was the decision to begin building an extermination camp at Belzec. At a meeting on October 17, Globocnik, Frank, and others agreed that the Lublin area should be cleared of Jews. Although they talked about "Jews being transferred across the Bug River," it is clear—since all participants knew by then that such deportations were impossible—that the "transfer" was a euphemism for murder.[41]

What remains in dispute is exactly what the camp's remit was. The rather limited initial scale of the construction may indicate that Belzec was more of an experiment than part of a comprehensive murder program. Belzec consisted of a few wooden buildings, staffed until the arrival of former euthanasia personnel in November by only three SS people. On the other hand, even camps that were quite small would prove capable of murdering extraordinarily large numbers of people, so the camp's size is not immediate proof of modest ambitions. At the very least, the murder of the hundreds of thousands of Lublin Jews was being contemplated. But there is some evidence that the authorities in the Generalgouvernement as a whole were now assuming that the Jewish population throughout that area would soon all be eliminated. In other words, even if the creation of the Belzec camp represents merely a response to Globocnik's initiative in Lublin, it seems possible that expectations within the wider Generalgouvernement were rapidly focusing on the murder of Polish Jews.[42]

THE CRYSTALLIZATION OF GENOCIDE

The thrust of recent research, then, is to suggest that the transition from murderously neglectful and brutal occupation policies to genocidal measures occurred initially without a comprehensive set of commands from the top. The leadership, above all Himmler, was consulted in almost all the cases we have looked at. But neither Hitler nor Himmler provided a clear-cut plan or even a basic command for the lower echelons to carry out.

What precisely was the role of Hitler, Himmler, and Heydrich in these months? Without Hitler, none of the developments would have materialized. It was Hitler who foregrounded the agenda of antisemitism and, just as important, imposed the fundamental terms of warfare and occupation. The failure of humanitarian impulses to exercise any restraint on the regime's activity was due to him. Perhaps the last check fell when Hitler expressly overruled the army's humanitarian concerns in the Polish campaign.[43] Every action taken against Jews by lower-level officials was legitimated by their knowledge of Hitler's own radical antisemitic agenda. Hitler's public pronouncements against Jews were legion.[44] He repeatedly returned, for example, to his "prophecy."[45] Whatever Hitler's precise intentions, his rhetoric thus provided the justification for others' actions, assuring the perpetrators that murder was appropriate.

Moreover, though the evidence is less clear here, the regime was so focused on Hitler that it seems likely that any initiatives on the Jewish question had his imprimatur. When, for example, Wilhelm Koppe, a senior SS commander in the Warthegau, asked Himmler if thirty thousand Poles suffering from TB could be killed, he was told that the Führer's approval was required.[46] Even where Hitler concealed his involvement, therefore, we know that authority lay with him. As the Serbian case shows, however, there is some question as to what his subordinates believed was already covered by their existing remit and what required new authorization. Many historians assume that in October 1941 Hitler gave approval for the killings of Warthegau Jews at Chelmno and for the construction of Belzec. There is no evidence of Hitler's direct involvement, but the way the system functioned makes it highly probable.

In contrast to Hitler's ambiguous intention in authorizing resumption of deportations in September, Heydrich's approach to them bordered on the genocidal from the start. The preparations of the Security Police in Lódz suggest that Heydrich always assumed that a large percentage of the deportees would die though not necessarily that they would be shot outright. The Gestapo planned to divide the ghetto into two sections, one for working Jews and a much smaller one for the larger number of nonworking Jews. The clear implication was that the latter group would die of hunger and disease. In October, once it was plain that Lodz would receive only a small share of the envisaged deportees, Heydrich looked to the Baltic and Byelorussia as additional destinations. At a meeting on the tenth, Heydrich proposed a particularly radical approach to the deportation of Czech Jews.[47] Those to be deported to Riga, in the Baltic, and to Minsk, in Byelorussia, should be the most burdensome Jews (*lästigste Juden*), that is, the least capable of working. Some historians believe that he assumed these Jews would be shot by the *Einsatzgruppen*.[48] More recently, Christian Gerlach has raised the possibility that the preparations for an extermination camp at Mogilev, in Byelorussia, where gassing experiments had taken place in September, may have had some connection to these deportations.[49] Whatever he intended exactly, Heydrich seems to have been thinking of very low survival rates: for the Czech Jews not on the first deportation lists, Heydrich planned to create separate ghettos for those able to work and those dependent on assistance (*Versorgungslager*), so that the Jewish communities would be decimated before they were even shoved onto the trains.[50]

In other words, even though there was not yet a precise concept of killing the deportees by gas, the dividing line between the territorial solution and that of outright murder was becoming very thin indeed. On October 23, all Jewish emigration from the Reich was prohibited. On the twenty-fifth, Erhard Wetzel, the official in charge of race questions in Rosenberg's Ministry for the Occupied Eastern Territories, wrote to the Reich commissioner for the Ostland (the Baltic), Hinrich Lohse, recommending the deployment of the former euthanasia personnel to construct gas installations for eliminating deported Jews who were unfit to work.[51] The "territorial" policy of sending the Jews east was becoming more and more of a metaphor. Selection and attrition were becoming the central elements of the process rather than desirable by-products.

In mid-November, Himmler and Rosenberg had a lengthy meeting, after which Rosenberg provided a detailed press briefing. Here the distance between deportation and destruction had narrowed to nothing. Though the issue of killing Jews—as against allowing them to die—was not yet spelled out and Rosenberg still spoke of deportation, his reference to the "biological eradication of the entire Jewry of Europe" made absolutely explicit that the Reich's aim was the extinction, not just the removal, of the Jewish presence.[52] At almost exactly the same time, on November 16, in the journal *Das Reich,* Goebbels published a lead article that was excerpted in many of the German regional papers.[53] Entitled "The Jews Are Guilty," the piece provided one of the clearest communications to the German people that Jews were going to be exterminated. World Jewry, Goebbels wrote, was suffering a gradual process of annihilation. Jews were falling according to their own law—an eye for an eye, a tooth for a tooth. In December, Goebbels acknowledged in his diary that the deportation of Jews to the East was "in many cases synonymous with the death penalty."[54]

Although Hitler still occasionally spoke as though deportation to a reservation remained the policy, there are hints that he was now rejecting any kind of territorial solution. At a dinner with Himmler and Heydrich at his headquarters on October 25, 1941, Hitler referred to his prophecy and went on in characteristically ambiguous fashion:

> Let no one say to me we cannot send them into the swamp! Who takes any interest in *our* people? It is good if our advance is preceded by fear that we will exterminate Jewry. The attempt to create a Jewish state will end in failure.[55]

Hitler's reference to a swamp (*Morast*) suggests he knew of the efforts by the SS to drown Jewish women and children in the Pripet Marshes.[56]

Hitler's shift may have had something to do with his loss of interest in Jews as hostages, which, the historian Shlomo Aronson argues, occurred at around this time. Roosevelt's declaration on September 11 that the U.S. navy would shoot on sight Axis warships in waters essential for American defense was one turning point.[57] It is possible that Roosevelt's decision to extend Lend-Lease aid to Moscow on October 1 was the final straw.[58] In any case, on November 28, Hitler met with the Grand Mufti of Jerusalem. Hitler was seeking to court the Grand Mufti, who was no doubt aware that just a few years earlier the Nazis had been working together with Jewish agencies to "facilitate" Jewish emigration to Palestine. Some of what Hitler said will have been for effect. Still, Hitler's declaration, which he requested the Mufti to "lock deep into his heart," was striking.[59] To please the Grand Mufti, Hitler need only have specified that the Germans would deport the Jews to Siberia, much as he had told Croatian Marshal Slavko Kvaternik in the summer.[60] But he went much further. After a successful war, Hitler said, Germany would have only one remaining objective in the Middle East: the annihilation of the Jews living under British protection in Arab lands. Not even a shadow of a territorial solution remained.

Another index of the hardening of attitudes was the evolving treatment of the German Jewish deportees. Up to November 8, twenty thousand German, Austrian, and Czech Jews (and five thousand Gypsies) had been deported to Lodz. In response to the protests of the Lodz authorities, more than thirty thousand more were deported to Minsk, Kovno, and Riga in the course of the following three months. What happened to these Jews varied greatly. Those sent to Lodz were interned in the ghetto. Those dispatched to Minsk were similarly housed in ghettos—left empty by the murders of the previous inhabitants. Though living conditions were horrendous, indeed barely survivable, the deportees were not murdered. Train shortages meant that only seven of the eighteen Minsk transports planned for 1941 actually took place; the last left on November 19. The proposed camp in Riga was not yet ready, so in the following week, five transports were sent instead to Kovno, in Lithuania. All the occupants were murdered on arrival in the infamous Ninth Fort. The first deportees to Riga, arriving on November 30, were also massacred. Up to early December 1941, then, "only" six of the forty-one transports of Reich Jews had been murdered on arrival, and all the murders had taken place at the end of November.[61]

There is considerable debate as to the reason for these murders, particularly the killing of Berlin Jews in Riga. On November 29–30, just before the deportees' arrival, four thousand Latvian Jews in the Riga ghettos had been murdered on the order of the HSSPF in the Baltic, Friedrich Jeckeln, and the local head of the Security Police, Rudolf Lange. On November 30, Himmler telephoned Heydrich from the Führer's headquarters with the message "Jewish transports from Berlin. No liquidation."[62] The message was duly sent on to Riga—but too late: the Berlin deportees had been included in the shooting. The historian Richard Breitman discovered in the Public Records Office the British intercept of an angry message from Himmler to his HSSPF: "The Jews resettled into the territory of the Ostland are to be dealt with only according to the guidelines given by me and the Reich Security Main Office acting on my behalf. I will punish unilateral acts and violations."[63] On the one hand, it seems hard to reconcile such a message with a preestablished plan to murder German Jews. On the other, the lack of reaction to the murders in Kovno confirms the sense gained from Heydrich's instructions of October 10 that there was no particular concern about killing German Jews either. Murder was at the very least being tolerated; indeed, it seems that "policy drift" was deliberately being cultivated from above.

So why the angry telegram? Breitman believes it was a response to a specific issue—the inclusion in the transport of Jewish Iron Cross holders, who should have been sent to the "old-age ghetto" in Theresienstadt.[64] But the urgency with which Jeckeln was then summoned to Berlin for talks would appear to indicate that more was at stake. We know that Hitler and Himmler were intensely sensitive to issues of morale and public opinion. Or, as Goebbels put it just eight days earlier, the Führer "wants an energetic policy against the Jews that, however, does not cause us unnecessary difficulties."[65] The transports of German Jews to Minsk and the Baltic and their inclusion in the killing process had led to a large number of questions. Some officials, notably commissar Wilhelm Kube in Minsk, had expressed reluctance to kill

German Jews. Even though such qualms were demonstrably ineffective in stopping deportations, they were probably beginning to raise some concern in Berlin. We know from Bernhard Lösener, the expert on Jewish matters in the Ministry of the Interior, that rumors about the murders of the Berlin Jews at Riga were making the rounds there.[66] Probably Himmler and perhaps Hitler as well decided that it would be politic to have further consultations before proceeding to eliminate more German Jews.

What began as a Soviet experiment was thus disseminated and modified piecemeal, by improvisation and example, over the period from September to November 1941. Himmler and Heydrich were closely involved; Hitler's involvement is less well documented, though he would at the very least have known what was happening, and at the very least have decided not to prevent it. Himmler could not have stayed his course without Hitler's approving nod, though how emphatic that was we do not know. Statements made by Hitler, Himmler, and those around them in October and November show how rapidly the idea of a territorial solution was dissolving into metaphor. The territories were becoming holding bays for those condemned to death. Whatever Hitler's green light for deportations had meant in September, by the end of November the idea of a reservation had effectively disappeared. It was then, as we will see, that Himmler held a concerted series of consultations on the

Jewish issue. Once the overall concept of genocide had crystallized in the minds of Nazi leaders, other agencies had to be brought on board.

There is no unequivocal evidence for this chronology or for the relationship between the murderous decisions and murderous actions that it implies. We cannot definitively rule out the possibility that Hitler had already decided on genocide much earlier, in the summer of 1941, or, as some historians believe, that the final moment of decision took place only later—in December 1941 or even in the spring or early summer of 1942. But let us test our approach against the evidence of the Wannsee Conference itself.

4

THE MEETING

INVITATIONS TO A CONFERENCE

In November 1941, Reinhard Heydrich was at the height of his career. Born in Halle of musical parents—and a gifted violinist himself—he had grown up in the turbulent conditions of the 1920s. His family was hit hard by the political upheavals and economic crises that followed the First World War, and university study was out of the question. Having admired the navy as a child, Heydrich sought a career as a naval officer. But in 1931 that plan ended in disaster when his treatment of a former fiancée was (rather unfairly) deemed conduct unbecoming to an officer. Recruited by Himmler to run his fledgling intelligence service, the SD, Heydrich rose rapidly. A driven and demanding man, he was something of a charismatic figure. An enthusiastic fencer, he was also a trained pilot and rather recklessly took time from his job to fly a Messerschmitt ME-109 in the attack on Norway in

April 1940. In September 1941, Heydrich finally came out from Himmler's shadow, when Hitler appointed him deputy (and de facto acting) protector for the occupied Czech territory. In typical Nazi style, Heydrich did not give up his existing position but merely added the new one, commuting regularly between Prague and Berlin. With a mixture of ruthlessness and a degree of flexibility, Heydrich soon made his mark in the Czech Protectorate. At the time of the Wannsee Conference, Heydrich was thus head of the Reichssicherheitshauptamt (the Reich Security Main Office, combining the Gestapo, the criminal police, and the SD for the whole of Germany), Reich protector in the occupied Czech territory, and one of the most feared and powerful men in Germany. He was thirty-seven.[1]

Heydrich's assistant, who would do much of the donkeywork for the Wannsee Conference, was a far less colorful character. Indeed, it was Adolf Eichmann's lack of stature or demonic quality at Jerusalem that led Hannah Arendt to coin the concept of the "banality of evil." Born in Solingen and of modest background, Eichmann apprenticed as a salesman in the 1920s, afterward working for an oil company in Linz. In 1933 he moved back to Germany and trained in the armed SS until the SD offered him the chance to display his bureaucratic talents. At first a relatively lowly official, he got his break in 1938 with the establishment of the Office for Jewish Emigration in Vienna. Here Eichmann demonstrated the combination of energy, ruthlessness, and ability to extract compliance from the Jewish officials under him that was to be his hallmark. When the RSHA was created, Eichmann became head of its Jewish section and was one of the principal organizers of the attempted transports of German Jews. At the time of the conference he was thirty-five.

Toward the end of November 1941, Heydrich had Eichmann draft some rather wordy invitations:[2]

On July 31, 1941, the Reich Marshal of the Greater German Reich commissioned me, with the assistance of the other central authorities, to make all necessary organizational and technical preparations for a comprehensive solution of the Jewish question and to present him with a comprehensive proposal at an early opportunity. A photocopy of his instructions is attached to this letter.

Given the extraordinary significance of these questions and in the interest of achieving a common view among the central agencies involved in the relevant tasks, I propose to hold a meeting on these issues. This is all the more important because since October 15, 1941, transports of Jews from the Reich territory, including the Protectorate of Bohemia and Moravia, have been regularly evacuated to the East. I therefore invite you to a meeting . . .

The invitations went out between November 29 and December 1. The meeting, followed by a buffet, was to be held on December 9 at an address given as the "Offices of

Interpol, 16 Am Kleinen Wannsee."[3] A subsequent memo, dated December 4, altered the venue to an SD guest house, 56-58 Am Grossen Wannsee.[4]

What clarification was needed on the Jewish question? What kind of preparations needed still to be made? We do not have much evidence of Heydrich's thinking in these days, but we do have the names he put on his guest list.[5] Whom had he invited and why were they there?

Heydrich's guests were important men, for the most part of status (though not of power) equal to his own. Most were *Staatssekretäre, Unterstaatssekretäre*, or the party equivalents thereof, ranks analogous to undersecretary of state in the United States or permanent secretary in the British civil service or their respective deputies.[6] "Those were the gentlemen," as prosecutor Robert Kempner reminded one of the many truculent Wannsee participants after the war who claimed to have known nothing about anything, "who knew the things you had to know."[7] Kempner had good reason to be confident of his judgment—in the Weimar era he had been a rising civil servant himself before fleeing to the United States. After 1933, the *Staatssekretäre*, if anything, increased in importance. With the cabinet disabled in the Third Reich and Hitler practically forbidding his ministers to meet independently, it was the fifty or so *Staatssekretäre* who were the essential medium of policy coordination. When new organizations like the Four Year Plan emerged, for example, they "borrowed" *Staatssekretäre* from the relevant ministries to act as coordinators. Meetings between the *Staatssekretäre* were in effect a substitute for cabinet government.

Heydrich's first list of names comprised two main groups. The largest was the representatives of ministries with responsibilities for the Jewish question, including men from the Ministries of the Interior, Justice, Economics, and Propaganda, the Reich Chancellery, the Foreign Office, and the Ministry for the Occupied Eastern Territories. The other invitees were all from party and SS agencies with a special interest in race questions: the Party Chancellery, the SS Main Office for Race and Settlement, and the Office of the Reich Commissar for the Strengthening of Germandom.

Looking at these candidates, we can immediately rule out the idea sometimes still voiced that Heydrich was planning to talk about the technical details of transports.[8] The problem of finding destinations for transports was undoubtedly pressing. Lodz's intake had been sharply reduced, Minsk had been shut down for a while, and Riga was delayed as a reception center. But quite apart from the fact that the *Staatssekretäre* were too senior to be called together for such matters, Heydrich had not invited any transport specialist or military representative or indeed anyone from the Ministry of Finance. Clearly, deportation arrangements were not to be on the agenda.

Many of Heydrich's original guests were involved in determining the status of Jews and dealing with the cases of

Mischlinge (the Nazi-invented category of mixed-race Jews) and mixed marriages. Indeed, for some of his proposed guests—the Party Chancellery representative and the Justice Ministry's man—such status questions were their principal point of involvement with the Jewish question. The guest list suggests, then, that the *Mischlinge* and borderline cases were to be high on the agenda.[9]

The historian Christian Gerlach has recently argued that the list was initially restricted to parties interested specifically in German Jews and only later gained a European dimension, and that this shift adds credence to his view that Hitler committed himself to genocide on a European scale only in December 1941. It is certainly true that the representative for occupied Poland was added as an afterthought.[10] On November 28, before the invitations went out but after the provisional list had been drawn up, Heydrich and Himmler were visited by the police and SS chief in the Generalgouvernement, Friedrich-Wilhelm Krüger, who bemoaned his difficulties with Governor Frank over spheres of jurisdiction. Only at that point did Heydrich decide to invite to his meeting civilian and Security Police representatives from Poland.[11]

It is indeed interesting that these representatives were not on his initial list. Whatever else Heydrich originally had in mind, it was clearly not a detailed discussion of the murder arrangements that were soon to fall into place in the Generalgouvernement. Yet we should not read too much into the additions, which were made very soon after the guest list was first drawn up. No one else with responsibility outside the Reich was subsequently added (though some of Heydrich's own staff at the meeting did have responsibilities outside Germany, and it is possible they were brought in only in December).[12] In any case, the initial list included delegates with international interests—two from the Ministry for the Occupied Eastern Territories as well as one from the Foreign Office. What the Krüger affair indicates rather more strongly is that Heydrich was particularly concerned to invite representatives of departments with whom he and Himmler had experienced difficulty. Resolving demarcation disputes and streamlining responsibilities were near the top of his agenda.

Many of the invitees were unsure what Heydrich wanted. For some, any kind of summons from the RSHA was a cause for dread. Since there was no agenda beyond the wording of the invitation itself, all sorts of interpretations were possible. The Ministry of the Interior had had the instructive experience not long before of sending a delegate to a meeting organized by Eichmann, only to find the agenda far broader than the one proposed.[13] Still, on this occasion the ministry thought it knew what was pending. One of its representatives, Werner Feldscher, informed a counterpart in the Ministry for the Occupied Eastern Territories that the Wannsee Conference had been called to achieve a "breakthrough" on the treatment of mixed-race Jews. A few days later, the

Interior Ministry's expert on Jewish questions drew up a paper in anticipation of a challenge to existing guidelines.[14] Feldscher, however, evidently believed that the meeting would discuss proposals for resolution of the Jewish question to be achieved only *after* the war, showing that he was far from up to speed on current thinking. For his part, Martin Luther, who ran the German department for the Foreign Office, believed the conference had a quite different scope, as a "wish list" drawn up on December 8 makes clear.[15] The Foreign Office clearly expected to be discussing the collection and deportation of Jews in countries all across Europe.[16]

POSTPONEMENT

The *Staatssekretäre* had longer to guess what awaited them than they might have expected. On December 8 Heydrich's staff telephoned round, deferring the meeting indefinitely.[17] Word of the Japanese attack on Pearl Harbor had reached Germany the evening before and it seems almost certain that this news was what put the gathering on hold. For one thing, the policy implications would need to be considered. After Japan had declared war against the United States, it was known that Hitler wanted to follow suit and enjoy the psychological advantage of beating the United States to the door. Hitler's declaration would involve calling a special Reichstag session; a number of the participants, including Heydrich himself, were members of the Reichstag and were likely to have to attend.[18] The other factor delaying the conference was probably the sudden dramatic worsening of conditions on the eastern front in early December. For the moment, the future of any eastern policy was in doubt.

It was now, in early December, Christian Gerlach argues, that Hitler finally decided to murder all European Jews. On December 12, at a meeting of Reich and district leaders of the Nazi Party, Hitler made some very strong statements (if Goebbels's diary provides an accurate record):

> As regards the Jewish question, the Führer has decided to sweep the floor clean. He prophesied to the Jews that if they ever caused a world war again, they would suffer extermination. This was not just mere phrasemaking. The world war is upon us; the extermination of the Jews is the necessary consequence. This question should be regarded without any sentimentality. We are here not to sympathize with the Jews but to sympathize with our German people. With the German people having once more sacrificed 160,000 dead in the campaign in the East, the original agents of this bloody conflict must pay with their lives.[19]

This pithy and hard-edged version of Hitler's prophecy followed one day after his Reichstag declaration of war against the United States. Four days later, one of those present, Hans Frank, gave a speech at an official meeting in the Generalgouvernement, in which he reiterated his desire for the Jews to be pushed east. A large Jewish migration would begin, he said:

> But what shall we do with the Jews? Do you think they are going to be settled in new villages in the West? They said to us in Berlin: Why cause us all this bother, we too have no use for them in the Baltic or in the Reich Commissariat, liquidate them yourselves! . . . These 3.5 million Jews—we can't shoot them, we can't poison them, but we will have to take steps to destroy them somehow, above all in connection with the measures to be discussed in the Reich.[20]

Seldom had any German official indicated more clearly that transport to the East meant murder.

Alongside these echoes of Hitler's message to the faithful, there are other clues that some decisive change had taken place. A memorandum dated December 16 from Alfred Rosenberg, the Reich minister for the occupied eastern territories, concerns a meeting with Hitler two days earlier. Rosenberg had drafted a major foreign policy speech and Hitler had evidently responded that Japan's entry into the war had changed the situation. Rosenberg noted,

> On the Jewish question I said that now, after the decision, the references to the New York Jews should perhaps be altered. I took the view that we should not talk about the destruction [*Ausrottung*] of the Jews. The Führer

agreed and said that they had imposed the war on us, they had brought destruction, so it should be no wonder if the consequences hit them first.[21]

It is not entirely clear what Rosenberg and Hitler had intended for the New York Jews, but Gerlach argues that the "decision" referred to was the murder of Europe's Jews.

Finally, there is an entry in Himmler's appointment calendar following a meeting with Hitler on December 18: "Judenfrage | als Partisanen auszurotten" ("Jewish question | to be eliminated as partisans"). Gerlach sees here a generic commitment to murdering Jews, particularly when taken in the context of other meetings and remarks around the same time.

Given the fluctuating character of Hitler's pronouncements, the fragments in themselves cannot be conclusive. When compared with his comments to Goebbels in August 1941, his comments to Himmler and Heydrich in October, or his subsequent remarks in 1942, those in December seem less obviously to define *the* moment of clarity. Hitler gave his speech just a day after the decision to wage war on the United States. At such moments, he was at his most vehement—as when, for example, he learned back in September of the Soviets' deportation of Volga Germans and gave the go-ahead for the deportations of German Jews. In January, however, Hitler's table talk reverted to ambiguity. On January 25, 1942, for example, he declared that "the Jew must leave Europe," warning that if the Jew chose not to emigrate, there would be extermination (and this after emigration had been stopped!).[22] On January 27, he was once again using the language—the metaphor?—of deportation: "The Jew must leave Europe! The best thing would be for them to go to Russia." A few days later he was more obscure: the Jew had to "disappear" from Europe.[23] Viewed over time Hitler's position would seem to shift discernibly from autumn 1941 onward, but the thinking is too erratic and fluctuates too much to provide clear or singular turning points. On the other hand, we know that even in his small circle of close advisers Hitler would sometimes pretend to certain views or knowledge. There is no proof, therefore, that when he talked of deportations he in fact thought Jews were not being killed.[24]

Our uncertainty about Hitler's thoughts, however, would not matter if we could show that his *subordinates* were sure they had heard the decisive word. Himmler's note about partisans seems far too fragmentary to be proof of anything, particularly since supporting arguments involving meetings with the leading euthanasia figures Bouhler and Brack are themselves circumstantial. Rosenberg's memo lends itself to the view that murder was already on the agenda before December. Rosenberg himself claimed at the Nuremberg trials that the "decision" he mentioned referred to Germany's entering the war against the United States, and in the German text this does seem a plausible reading.[25] An abstract concept like "The Decision" belonged to the language of fate and destiny with which the Nazis typically referred to war. And in Nazi thinking, there was a certain logic in the idea that, while open threats might have deterred the Jewish enemy from taking on Germany before the declaration of war, now the threats had no teeth. In short, Rosenberg's comments can be taken to mean that a preexisting policy of extermination should be dealt with differently in public rhetoric now that the war with America had begun.[26]

The memo does confirm, however, how much farther down the road to genocide Hitler had traveled since his September decision to resume deportations. Though Hitler had probably long since given up on influencing Roosevelt, the declaration of war closed the chapter (some dismal wartime negotiations notwithstanding) of using the Jews as diplomatic hostages. Up until this point, moreover, Hitler had tended to reserve his strongest remarks for his absolutely closest aides. But now he was addressing some fifty of his top lieutenants. This was a major event. His statement was bound to clarify the authority with which Himmler and Heydrich pushed forward their murderous vision. Party officials now had a more emphatic sense than ever of the leadership's commitment to murder.

On January 8, Heydrich sent a note to the Wannsee invitees expressing regret at the previous postponement. The explanation offered was hardly enlightening—"events which suddenly intruded and the resulting commitments of some of the invited participants." Heydrich now proposed meeting on January 20.[27] The conference had thus been deferred for almost six weeks. Did this indicate, as Eberhard Jäckel suggests, that the event was relatively unimportant? Heydrich's note talked rather of the urgency of the issues involved. The lengthy delay was more likely a reflection of the protracted period of uncertainty on the eastern front and the lack of spare transport capacity (though that problem would continue until March). By January 8, though the military situation remained critical the Germans could at least hope to soon restore their position.[28] Plans for deportation and murder could go ahead.

A VILLA IN WANNSEE

Wannsee is a beautiful suburb to the southwest of Berlin. Largely undeveloped until the mid-nineteenth century, the area prospered when the banker Wilhelm Conrad decided to build luxurious dwellings for wealthy Berliners seeking relief from the summer heat of the capital. In the latter decades of the nineteenth century, its rich villas and exotic gardens became the preferred summer residences of Berlin's upper middle class. From October to Easter, Wannsee slumbered peacefully, but in the summer months it filled with bankers and industrialists, scientists and artists. Ironically, given its later connotations, the name of Wannsee was then associated with cosmopolitanism and tolerance. Christians and acculturated or converted German Jews lived reasonably

comfortably side by side. Their afterlife was similarly har-
monious: both faiths were buried in the same cemetery, the
Neue Friedhof, whose walls bear both a cross and a Star of
David. The architect responsible for the Wannsee Conference villa also designed the house of one of Weimar's most
progressive spirits, the artist Max Liebermann. Living just a
stone's throw away from what would become one of the most
notorious addresses in the world, Liebermann, a leading
Impressionist and president of the Prussian Academy of
Arts, epitomized the tolerant and liberal-minded "other"
Germany.[29]

After 1933, Wannsee's beauty and tranquillity attracted
a string of leading Nazis. Josef Goebbels, Walther Funk,
Hermann Esser, Wilhelm Stuckart—one of Heydrich's
invitees—Hitler's doctor, Theo Morell, and many other Nazi
luminaries acquired properties. Like many of them, Albert
Speer bought his villa on the cheap at the expense of its Jewish owners. A number of Nazi organizations and foundations
also purchased properties. The Nazi Women's League established its Reich Bride School there; the National Socialist
Welfare ran a training school in one of the villas. The SS set
up several institutes in the area and the SD had been holding
conferences there since 1936.

The villa at 56-58 Am Grossen Wannsee enjoyed a mar-
velous view over the larger of the two Wannsee lakes, on whose
western shore it lay. It had belonged to Friedrich Minoux, a
right-wing industrialist with the Stinnes Company.[30] In 1940,

under investigation for fraud, Minoux sold the villa to an SD charitable foundation, the Stiftung Nordhav. The foundation's purpose was ostensibly to create holiday and convalescent homes for SD members, though it seems possible that its aim was also to acquire properties on Heydrich's behalf. After Minoux handed the house over in May 1941, the residence was converted into a guest house for senior Security Police and SD personnel visiting Berlin.[31]

In selecting the villa for the meeting, Heydrich eschewed more intimidating or businesslike locations in favor of an expansive and informal atmosphere. The guest house's promotional brochure promised "completely refurbished guest rooms, a music room and games room (billiards), a large meeting room and conservatory, a terrace looking out onto the Wannsee, central heating, hot and cold running water, and all comforts. The house offers good food, including lunch and dinner. Wine, beer, and cigarettes are available." For all of which the cost was a very reasonable 5RM per night, including service and breakfast.[32]

HEYDRICH'S GUESTS

On a snowy Tuesday morning, January 20, 1942, some fifteen senior officials gathered at the SD villa by the Wannsee lake.[33] Not everyone on Heydrich's original invitation list had come. The Propaganda Ministry's representative must have been unavoidably engaged, since the ministry expressed

a burning interest in participating in follow-up meetings.[34]
Ulrich Greifelt, the director of the Office of the Reich Commissar for the Strengthening of Germandom, also failed to
show; he may have been on business in Italy. The invitees
originally proposed from the Generalgouvernement had been
replaced by their subordinates. On the civilian side, it was
Hans Frank's deputy, Josef Bühler, who attended, while the
head of the Security Police for the Generalgouvernement,
Eberhard Schöngarth, came as Security Police representative
for the area.[35] The Justice Ministry's Franz Schlegelberger,
though *Staatssekretär* in rank, was acting minister at the
time, so he sent a deputy, Roland Freisler, later to serve as the
infamous president of the People's Court.

As noted earlier, the largest group around the table com-
prised the representatives of ministries with responsibilities
for the Jewish question: Wilhelm Stuckart (Interior), Roland
Freisler (Justice), Erich Neumann (Four Year Plan), Friedrich-
Wilhelm Kritzinger (Reich Chancellery), Martin Luther
(Foreign Office). The two representatives of the Ministry for
the Occupied Eastern Territories, Alfred Meyer and Georg
Leibbrandt, fell into this category as well, but, together with
Josef Bühler from the Generalgouvernement, they formed a
second group, namely German agencies with responsibilities
for civilian administration of occupied territories in the East.
Then there were the officials from the SS and the party with
special interest in race questions: Gerhard Klopfer (Party
Chancellery) and Otto Hofmann (SS Main Office for Race

and Settlement). Finally, in addition to the invitees, Heydrich had instructed officials from his own security empire to attend. The most senior was Heydrich's direct subordinate, the Gestapo chief Heinrich Müller, and below him, Adolf Eichmann. From the field there were Eberhard Schöngarth of the Generalgouvernement and Rudolf Lange, the head of *Einsatzkommando* 2 and regional chief for the Security Police in Riga. It is possible that Eichmann's deputy, Rolf Günther, was present to take notes.

These were influential and, for the most part, well-educated men. Two-thirds had university degrees, and over half bore the title of doctor, mainly of law. They were also strikingly young. Almost half were under forty, only two were fifty or older. Youth was particularly apparent among the party, SS, and Security Police representatives, five of whom were in their thirties. Yet even on the civilian side, ambitious young men were not lacking. Wilhelm Stuckart, perhaps the most important man in the Ministry of the Interior given the ineffectiveness of the minister, Wilhelm Frick, was only thirty-nine.

With what expectations and feelings did the assembled gentlemen enter Minoux's former villa that day? Those who survived the war and were brought to trial in the immediate postwar years denied having attended at all. After the protocol was found they affected only faint recollection. Adolf Eichmann spoke more openly, but his testimony is unreliable, particularly on his own aspirations, concerned as he was to portray himself as dutiful errand boy, with neither initiative nor knowledge. Although we can only guess what he and the others felt, we can be fairly certain that they did not all come with the same spirit or expectations. Heydrich's men and his guests from the SS and the party hoped that the meeting would further radicalize the Jewish agenda and wrest power from the ministries. The ministries were by and large on the defensive, seeking to protect their waning influence from further incursions by the Security Police. Of all the participants, Wilhelm Stuckart had most cause to feel beleaguered. He would have suspected, quite rightly, that one of the meeting's functions was to subordinate the civilian agencies, and above all his own ministry, to the insistent claims of Heydrich's RSHA.

THE PROTOCOL

Before the meeting convened, Eichmann testified, the assembled men stood around in groups and chatted for a while. Then they got down to business. The actual proceedings were relatively short—perhaps an hour to an hour and a half. With no formal agenda, much of the time was taken up by an extensive lecture from Heydrich. It seems there were some interjections from the other participants and a little more discussion afterward. But these are conjectures; we have no direct transcript of what was said. A stenotypist took minutes in shorthand (it is probably Eichmann's invention that a second SS official, his deputy, Rolf Günther, also recorded the proceedings), but the notes have not been preserved. In any case, they were not verbatim notes, according to Eichmann, but a record only of the salient points.[36] What we have is the protocol, or Eichmann's gloss on the notes, which he claimed were in turn heavily edited by Heydrich.

The protocol is thus very far from a word-for-word account. "These weren't records," Heinrich Lammers, the head of the Reich Chancellery, protested at Nuremberg. "They're just one-sided minutes, compiled in the RSHA."[37] For our purposes, that distinction does not really matter. The protocol reflects the aims and interests of the man who called the meeting—Reinhard Heydrich—and is in many ways as important as anything he actually said that day. Perhaps more so, since the protocol represents what he wanted written down and recorded. When the participants received it, they learned what it was he wished them to know, whether or not it accorded with their own memory of what had been discussed. For this reason, some of the civil servants' postwar denials that murder had been discussed at the meeting are beside the point. Perhaps not surprisingly, no one dared submit criticisms or amendments to Heydrich, though internal memos in the ministries suggested that on at least one matter the outcome of the discussion had been less conclusive than the protocol indicated.[38] So, while the protocol gives us a good idea of Heydrich's message, it is less useful in identifying the role the other participants played at the meeting, and their response to what they heard. We can glean some clues from the document and others from postwar testimony, but that is all.

According to the protocol, Heydrich began by reminding his guests that Göring, the Reich marshal, had entrusted him with preparing the final solution of the European Jewish question.[39] The purpose of the present meeting was to establish clarity on fundamental questions. The Reich marshal's desire to be provided with an outline of the organizational, policy, and technical prerequisites for the final solution of the European Jewish question made it necessary to ensure in advance that the central organizations involved were brought together and their policies properly coordinated.[40] Overall control of the final solution lay, irrespective of geographical boundaries, with the Reichsführer-SS and chief of the German police (that is, Himmler) and specifically with Heydrich as his representative.

Heydrich then reminded his listeners of the recent history of Nazi action against the Jews. The principal goals had been to remove Jews from different sectors of German society and then from German soil. The only solution available at the time had been to accelerate Jewish emigration, a policy that led in 1939 to the creation of the Reich Central Office for Jewish Emigration. The disadvantages of a policy of emigration were clear to all those involved, he said, but in the absence of alternatives the policy had to be tolerated, at least initially. But the Reichsführer-SS had now stopped emigration in view of the dangers it posed during wartime and the new possibilities in the East.

Instead of emigration, Heydrich continued, the Führer had given his approval for a new kind of solution—the evacuation of Jews to the East. The next, ambiguous sentence reads, "These actions are nevertheless to be seen only as temporary relief [*Ausweichmöglichkeiten*] but they are providing the practical experience that is of great significance for the coming final solution of the Jewish question." With breathtaking calmness, the protocol continues with the observation that around eleven million Jews would be affected by the final solution. A table was provided listing European countries and their Jewish populations; it included not only those countries under German occupation or control (part A) but also Germany's European allies, neutral countries, and those with whom it was still at war (part B). These figures, Heydrich noted, had had to be drawn from statistics of religious affiliation, since a number of the countries involved lacked a proper racial census. Some miscellaneous remarks followed about the difficulty of tackling the Jewish question in Romania and Hungary and about the occupational composition of Jews in Russia. Whether Eichmann's protocol was just picking up fragments here, or Heydrich was responding to questions, or his presentation really did consist of such little snippets, we do not know. Then came one of the most significant sections:

In the course of the final solution and under appropriate leadership, the Jews should be put to work in the East. In large, single-sex labor columns, Jews fit to work will work their way eastward constructing roads. Doubtless the large majority will be eliminated by natural causes. Any final remnant that survives will doubtless consist of the most resistant elements. They will have to be dealt with appropriately, because otherwise, by natural selection, they would form the germ cell of a new Jewish revival. (See the experience of history.)

Germany proper and the Czech Protectorate would be cleared first and then Europe would be combed from West to East. Bit by bit the Jews would be brought to transit ghettos and then transported farther east.

Heydrich next identified some key prerequisites for the deportations (or "evacuations," in the language of the protocol). There had to be clarity about who was going to be deported. Jews over sixty-five and those who had suffered serious injuries or received the Iron Cross First Class in World War I would be sent to Theresienstadt. At a stroke, this would obviate the many anticipated interventions on their behalf. The larger evacuation actions would begin when the military situation allowed. There followed a discussion about the situation in countries allied with Germany or under its influence—Slovakia, Croatia, Italy, France, and so on. Southeastern Europe and Western Europe would raise no particular problems, Martin Luther of the Foreign Office assured the other representatives, but caution would be necessary in approaching the Scandinavian countries. In view of the small number of Jews involved, deferring Jewish measures in Scandinavia would not be a major problem.

A lengthy discussion of the issue of half Jews and mixed marriages was next, taking up almost a third of the minutes, a clear indication of its importance to Heydrich. He called for first-degree *Mischlinge* (persons with two Jewish grandparents, or "half Jews") to be evacuated to the East with the rest of the Jews. There would be a few exceptions, and in those cases the person concerned should be sterilized. Representing the SS Race and Settlement Office, Otto Hofmann argued that "extensive use should be made of sterilization, particularly as the *Mischling,* presented with the choice of evacuation, would rather submit to sterilization." As for Jews in mixed marriages, Heydrich said that a decision should be made on a case-by-case basis as to whether the Jewish partner should be evacuated or, in view of the impact of such a measure on the German relatives, be sent to a so-called old-age ghetto, such as Theresienstadt.

The last part of the minutes records a number of interventions by various participants. Possibly the protocol grouped together individual comments that had been made in the course of the meeting and inserted them here. During cross-examination in Jerusalem, however, Eichmann indicated that toward the end of the meeting, and somewhat fortified by brandy, the participants turned what had been a monologue by Heydrich into a bit of a free-for-all.[41] Erich Neumann from the Four Year Plan organization said that Jews should not be removed from essential enterprises unless replacement labor could be provided. Heydrich agreed, pointing out that this was already the policy. Josef Bühler from the Generalgouvernement asked that the final solution begin in Poland, since there were no major transport or manpower problems. The paraphrase of his argument in the protocol continues:

> The Jews must be removed from the territory of the Generalgouvernement as quickly as possible because of the particular danger there of epidemics being brought on by Jews. Jewish black-market activities were persistently destabilizing the region's economy. The 2½ million Jews in the region were in any case largely unable to work.

The authorities in the Generalgouvernement accepted Heydrich's primacy in all matters pertaining to the Jewish question, Bühler said, and would support his work. Bühler "had only one request—that the Jewish question be solved as quickly as possible."

An ominous section at the very end of the protocol notes that "in conclusion the various possible kinds of solution were discussed." A rather obscure sentence adds that both Bühler and Alfred Meyer of the Ministry for the Occupied

Eastern Territories felt that certain preparations for the final solution should be carried out immediately in the territories concerned, though without alarming the populace.[42] With a final request for cooperation and assistance in carrying out his tasks, Heydrich closed the meeting. Afterward, Eichmann testified, the guests stood around in small groups for a little while, then left.

WHAT THE *STAATSSEKRETÄRE* LEARNED

The Jews, the *Staatssekretäre* heard, were to be "evacuated to the East." Did this phrase mean the transportation of the Jewish population to a more eastern location? It is a staple of Holocaust deniers that it does. But serious historians, too, in questioning the absence of explicit references to murder, have raised doubts about whether Wannsee established that the Jews were to be killed. True, Eichmann said several times in Jerusalem that the language used on January 20 had been more open about killings than the protocol suggests. Such an admission fit in with Eichmann's defense strategy, which was to establish that his superiors had given clear killing orders.[43] The testimony of the ministerial bureaucrats at the Nuremberg trials was very different. Their defense was to claim they had known nothing of the Jews' fate, and they thus denied that anything had been said openly.[44] Wilhelm Stuckart, having at first professed barely to remember attending the conference, responded in cross-examination:

No, I don't believe that I am wrong in saying that there was no
   discussion of the final solution of the Jewish question, in the
   sense in which it is now understood.
KEMPNER: Heydrich related clearly, in your presence, what it
   was about?
STUCKART: That is absolutely out of the question—otherwise
   I would have known what it meant.[45]

Friedrich-Wilhelm Kritzinger from the Reich Chancellery was alone among those cross-examined by Robert
Kempner after the war in expressing feelings of shame.[46] Yet
he, too, denied killings had been openly talked about, a fact
that has led eminent historians such as Hans Mommsen and
Dieter Rebentisch to accept that claim.[47] Wilhelm Stuckart's
subordinate, Bernhard Lösener, by contrast, maintained after
the war that "at the notorious Wannsee Conference, at the
latest, . . . Stuckart gained precise information."[48]

Two separate matters are in danger of being confused
here. One is the question of whether the Wannsee protocol
clearly envisaged the killing of all Jews. The other is whether
it clearly determined and articulated the *means* of killing. On
the former question, the evidence is straightforward. Otto
Hofmann was sure that half Jews could be relied upon to
prefer sterilization if the alternative was "evacuation." Heydrich argued that because of the psychological impact on the
German relatives the Jewish partner in mixed marriages
might be deported to a ghetto rather than "evacuated."

What kind of "evacuation" could they have been talking about? "One thing is clear," concluded the judges in the Ministries Trial at Nuremberg, "no one would suggest sterilization as a procedure of amelioration unless he was wholly convinced that deportation meant a worse fate, namely, death."[49]

But the protocol is even more revealing than that. With ice-cold precision, Heydrich clarified that even Jews fit for work were destined to die. Either they would be crushed by working conditions or murdered for being resilient enough to survive them. The fate of Jews deemed *unable* to work at the outset could hardly be open to doubt. Josef Bühler justified his request that the final solution begin in the Generalgouvernement with the argument that most of the Jews there were unable to work—another indication that the participants knew they were talking about murder.[50]

The protocol suggests that a comprehensive plan was just emerging. Heydrich refers to all previous policies as interim measures. The promotion of emigration, the regime's earlier policy, had been such a "provisional solution," Heydrich claimed. The more recent evacuation "actions" were also mere "temporary relief." (It is not absolutely clear whether Heydrich is referring here to ongoing or impending "actions," but the comment that they were providing "practical experience" of "great significance for the coming final solution of the Jewish question" suggests that Heydrich was referring to the ongoing deportations.) These comments, together with

Heydrich's invitation letter and the opening remarks in the protocol, convey a picture of a genocidal program only now taking shape. The new wave of deportations initiated in September had not yet been properly tied to a clear strategy for eliminating Jews. Those historians who believe the decision for genocide had been made long before have difficulty understanding Heydrich's remarks and effectively have to discount them. What he says makes sense, however, if viewed against the background of the crystallization of policy in the autumn of 1941.

What reason is there to believe Gerlach's view that the meeting's scope had been widened as a result of an ostensible Hitler decision in December to murder all European Jews? As already noted in relation to the guest list, the evidence is not very conclusive. At his trial, Eichmann indicated that he had carried out the preparatory work for Heydrich's speech in advance of the December deadline, not in January. He claimed to have gathered the statistics for Heydrich's broad survey of the European Jewish problem some two weeks before the original date.[51] Eichmann's references to dates are, of course, always to be regarded with caution. We know that he ordered the Reich Association of Jews to produce German statistics at the beginning of November and that he had already demanded European figures earlier in the summer, but it is hard to be certain exactly what he put together for Heydrich and when.[52]

More significant is that in his Jerusalem testimony about

Wannsee Eichmann made no reference to a decision by Hitler in December, though it would have been very much in his interest to do so. The protocol itself says merely that new possibilities of "evacuation" had emerged, not by Hitler's order but merely with the Führer's "prior approval." Such a cautious and rather passive account of Hitler's role is no surprise in the *written* protocol: it accorded with his desire not to be linked on paper to a murder order. But if Gerlach's emphasis on Hitler's decision of December 1941 were correct, we might have expected that *orally*, at least, Heydrich would have made stronger reference to the Führer's "decision"—and certainly that at his trial Eichmann would have remembered such a reference. After all, Eichmann's defense rested on the existence of unambiguous orders that he, as a mere underling, was simply carrying out. Yet Eichmann had nothing to say on the matter.[53] On balance, therefore, it seems that Heydrich had always planned to make a presentation with European dimensions, based on the decisions that had crystallized in October and November.

In another striking recent interpretation, the historian Peter Longerich challenges the idea that Wannsee expressed a commitment to anything beyond the deportation program unleashed by Hitler's decision in September 1941.[54] Longerich argues that the only difference was that it was now openly on the table that no one was intended to survive deportation for long. The conference, he points out, was not followed by any immediate decisions to expand the scale of the killing facilities. Instead, there was simply a notification from Eichmann at the end of January that the deportations were to be resumed as soon as transport bottlenecks allowed. In short, for Longerich, Wannsee was simply an occasion for the murderous rhetoric surrounding the deportations to be ratcheted up a notch. Yet in September, as we have seen, Hitler's green light was quite probably still linked to the idea of an eastern reservation. The temporary locations of Lodz and Minsk were holding bays before the populations could be sent farther east in the spring. To be sure, the whole process was already murderous enough, but that is different from genocide. By Wannsee it was clear all were to die. The reference to killing Jewish workers who survived the working conditions could scarcely have been more explicit. The "eastern" territory to which the Jews should be evacuated was now mere code.

The only open question is about the means of killing. Did Wannsee take place at a time when the Nazi leadership, though now committed to death rather than to a territorial solution of slow attrition, had not yet clearly decided the *actual method* of killing? Had they still to establish the balance between gassing Jews, shooting them, or starving and working them to death? Or did the protocol show that a fair measure of clarity existed on this topic as well? There are some indications that Heydrich *did* talk at the meeting about how the Jews would be murdered. There is the ominous reference in the minutes to the discussion of the various "kinds of solution" (*Lösungsmöglichkeiten*). Possibly Bühler's comment that transport would not be a problem in the Generalgouvernement implied awareness that extermination camps were being developed in Poland and that deportations into distant parts of the Soviet Union were no longer being considered.[55] Given Heydrich's comments about Jewish workers, it is certainly hard to imagine that he had not anticipated, and did not respond to, questions about how the Jews would be killed. Eichmann said in Jerusalem that they discussed the "business with the engine" and shooting, but not poison gas.[56] He may have been distinguishing here between killing by means of the internal combustion engine—the technique already used at Chelmno—and cyanide, a technique tried out at Auschwitz but not yet in general use.

Yet there is no hard and fast proof that the participants learned at the meeting that Jews were going to be gassed. Kritzinger and Stuckart, as we know, denied hearing such talk. In an entry in his official diary later in the war, Bühler's boss, Hans Frank, implied that he heard about the gassing of Jews only in the latter part of the war. This diary is itself unreliable. From 1943 on, Frank was mindful of being on the Allies' list of war criminals and conscious of the need to falsify the historical record.[57] After all, as far as we know, Frank had been involved in the discussions surrounding the construction of Belzec in 1941. Nevertheless, some doubt about Wannsee must remain.

But the point is worth making again: whether or not the

means were clearly established, the "final solution" now unambiguously meant the death of all European Jews. Except for the specific privileged exceptions to be deported to the so-called old-age ghetto at Theresienstadt (most of whom, as we know, were in any case sent on to Auschwitz), there was no other outcome than death. Any Jews who were not "eliminated by natural causes" would be "dealt with appropriately." Possibly the plan was not spelled out at the meeting itself—but that is of secondary importance; it was there, in black and white, in the protocol. At the latest, by the time it landed on their desks, Stuckart, Kritzinger, and all the rest knew what was intended.[58] Small wonder that in the Ministries Trial in 1948 both Stuckart and Kritzinger's boss, Heinrich Lammers, denied having received it. Lammers's denial was undermined by the fact that two years earlier, at Nuremberg, he had freely acknowledged having read the document (it contained "nothing new," he claimed at that point). Unfortunately for him, the protocol was then found by the Allies and its explosive contents were exposed. Stuckart's denial was equally implausible, since he had agreed to send a subordinate to a follow-up meeting, the invitations for which arrived at the same time as the protocol. But both men knew what they would be admitting if they acknowledged receipt.[59]

Heydrich's remarks shed light on the evolution not just of the Final Solution but also of Nazi attitudes to Jewish labor. Some of the ambiguities of Nazi policy at this time reflect the fact that just as deportation plans were being replaced by murder, the authorities were being confronted with manpower shortages on a new and dangerous scale.[60] Over the previous couple of years the use of Jewish labor reserves had been extremely haphazard and contradictory. In the Generalgouvernement, lip service had been paid in many quarters to the idea of distinguishing between productive Jews and others, and this distinction became the rationale for ever more concrete proposals about eliminating those unfit for work. But even those Jews designated as capable of working were not used effectively; payment, rations, and discipline were so horrific as to prevent rational exploitation of their labor. Working conditions on SS projects were an extended form of murder.[61]

In the Soviet Union, policy had moved back and forth. The early approach of the *Einsatzkommandos* was to emphasize "security" and disregard manpower, eliminating all Jewish men of working age. Exceptions were then introduced for key workers and the Wehrmacht made extensive use of Jewish labor. The pendulum began to swing back toward killing, however, and Himmler's men tried to restrict the use of Jewish labor. Where Jewish workers were indispensable, Himmler's men sought to bring them under their own control and deploy them in separate work columns. Toward the end of 1941, the Ministry for the Occupied Eastern Territories, responding to various inquiries, thus informed its subordinates that, in principle, economic considerations should be disregarded in eliminating Jews. But manpower shortages were becoming acute again, and there was renewed pressure to conserve labor. As a result of the manpower shortage, the number of shootings declined for a while.[62]

One attempt to reconcile the need for Jews and the wish to get rid of them was the emergence of an explicit concept of extermination through labor. In the Soviet Union, *Einsatzgruppe* C developed the idea of using Jews for construction projects in a way that would solve temporary labor shortages and at the same time wear out and kill the workers. In Galicia, Fritz Katzmann, the SS and police leader, developed the idea of employing Jewish workers under literally murderous conditions to reconstruct a major transit route.[63] Himmler himself began to think more actively about using Jewish labor in the concentration camps, and in January 1942 he readied the camps for a major influx of Jewish workers (which only partially materialized). It is against this background that we can understand Heydrich's remarks. Echoing Katzmann's lethal project, Heydrich attempted to balance the current labor scarcities with the desire to eliminate all Jews.[64] It is possible, as Hans Mommsen argues, that the fiction of rationally utilizing labor provided the psychological function of creating a bridge from the reservation policy to genocide.[65] But if Heydrich ever had needed such a psychological bridge, his willingness at Wannsee to kill off competent and resilient workers suggested that he had already crossed it.

CONTROLLING THE BOUNDARIES

The Wannsee Protocol is thus a kind of keyhole through which we can glimpse the emerging Final Solution. The meeting took place at a time when the idea of a reservation had been abandoned, labor scarcities were pressing, and the Nazis may or may not have decided on the exact method of eliminating the Jews. But it is quite evident that Wannsee is not the place where the decision for murder was taken. For the most part, Heydrich was disseminating conclusions arrived at elsewhere. On some issues, to be sure, the participants had something to say. Essentially their role was to listen and to nod.

Why then had he called them together? One of the few areas where there were still clear differences of principle, particularly between the ministries and the RSHA, was the question of how to deal with the borderline cases of half Jews and mixed marriages.[66] The Interior Ministry, as we know, felt in advance of the meeting that this issue was likely to be the key item on the agenda. Even after the war, State Secretary Stuckart still claimed that Heydrich had called the meeting primarily to remove obstacles to deporting half Jews and Jews in mixed marriages.[67]

The problem of defining who was a Jew had vexed the Nazis ever since they came to power. Early measures, such as the forced retirement of civil servants in 1933, used a broad definition, targeting those with even one Jewish grandparent. Party members had to prove the absence of Jewish fore-bears back to 1800, SS officials back to 1750. With the rein-troduction of conscription in 1935, however, the army was allowed to make exceptions and recruit half- and quarter-Jewish recruits—which it seems to have done with alacrity. Party radicals, though, were worried that precedents were being set that might lead to civil rights for half and quarter Jews. Their pressure for a definitive and far-reaching ruling helps explain Hitler's decision to announce citizenship and blood laws at the party rally in Nuremberg in September 1935.[68]

The history of the so-called Nuremberg Laws, and partic-ularly of the subsequent decrees defining their precise scope, reveals that, unlike "full Jews," half and quarter Jews had institutional champions, above all Stuckart's department in the Ministry of the Interior, with assistance from the Reich Chancellery. Why the Interior Ministry should have played this role is not clear. It may well have reflected a commit-ment on the part of Bernhard Lösener, Stuckart's expert on Jewish questions. Whatever the original motivation, once the Interior Ministry took on the cause of half and quarter Jews, ministerial prestige was at stake. Even Lösener's own postwar testimony, in which he was at pains to underline his anti-Nazi credentials, makes evident that the issue became a question as much of departmental amour propre as of moral principle.[69]

The other factor helping the half and quarter Jews was

Hitler's sensitivity to public morale. There were so many full-German relatives to consider. Ideologically, Hitler favored the hard line of the party radicals, but tactically he was hesitant.[70] A classic example is his behavior with regard to the Nuremberg Laws. When the Interior Ministry sought to add a clause stating that "these laws apply to full Jews only," Hitler allowed it to be included in the press release announcing the laws but had it deleted from the actual text.[71] His role was similarly equivocal in the drawn-out battle of definitions that followed promulgation of the Nuremberg Laws in September 1935.

Party radicals were by and large willing to exempt the quarter Jew but wanted to see half Jews designated as Jews, with a few exceptions individually sanctioned by the party. The Interior Ministry, by contrast, argued that the half German should be protected rather than the half Jew punished.[72] The compromise outcome was a new legal category, the *Mischling*, defined by a disparate muddle of religious and "racial" criteria. Quarter Jews were termed *Mischlinge* (so-called *Mischlinge* second degree) but were allowed to marry other Germans, though not other *Mischlinge* or Jews.[73] Half Jews were also considered *Mischlinge* (first degree) unless they were members of synagogues or had married Jews, in which case they were considered full Jews (*Geltungsjuden*).[74] The party's desire to be able to select which (few) half Jews might be tolerated had been rebuffed, but so had the Interior Ministry's blanket protection of the half Jew. The radicals did succeed in introducing a ruling that half Jews were forbidden from marrying quarter Jews or Germans, unless exceptions were allowed by Hitler. The only way they could maintain their status as *Mischlinge* was thus either to stay single or to marry another half Jew.[75]

The other key borderline issue was that of mixed marriages. The Nuremberg Laws, though they banned future unions between Jews and non-Jews, had had little to say about existing mixed marriages. At the end of 1938, however, after consulting with Hitler, Göring drew up guidelines distinguishing between "privileged mixed marriages" and the others. Privileged marriages were those where the man was non-Jewish, with the exception of marriages where there were children who had had Jewish educations. Marriages in which the husband was Jewish were not privileged, with the exception of those marriages in which there were Christian children (and the children were still living or had fallen in active service). If the Jewish partner was the wife, then the new controls on Jewish property affected her property only. When the yellow star was introduced, the concept of privileged marriages was extended to include Jews married to second-degree *Mischlinge* and even to Jews whose marriages had been terminated by divorce or death, provided they were the parents of a *Mischling* child (or had been and the child had been killed in action). Jews in such privileged marriages did not have to wear the star. The bizarre mixture of "racial," religious, and gender criteria, lacking any theoretical rationale, shows that the regime's fear of public reaction was the guiding principle.[76]

In 1941 party radicals renewed efforts to abolish the protected categories. A working group combining Walter Gross's Racial Policy Office and the new Institute for Research on the Jewish Question in Frankfurt, called for *Mischlinge* to be legally equated with Jews.[77] The RSHA, too, began to take a more active interest, particularly once it became important to define which groups should be deported from the Reich. On August 21, 1941, Eichmann convened a meeting at which the Party Chancellery, the Racial Policy Office, and the RSHA coordinated their positions. The demands they formulated were almost exactly those Heydrich put on the table at Wannsee.[78]

With an exception or two (notably the Führer Chancellery and the military), Heydrich had invited to the meeting all parties involved in decisions on half and quarter Jews. Heydrich now mounted a frontal assault on the compromises enacted since the Nuremberg Laws. First-degree *Mischlinge* were to be equated with full Jews. Only those with proven exceptional service to the state and party or with children who were second-degree *Mischlinge* could hope for better treatment, that is, "voluntary" sterilization. Even in relation to the second-degree *Mischlinge*, Heydrich's proposals breached the general understanding of protection. Second-degree *Mischlinge* whose parents were both first-degree *Mischlinge*, for example, or who *looked* racially unfavorable or who had particularly negative police or political records could be treated as Jews. Although these rules did not apply if the second-degree *Mischling* had married a German partner, they nevertheless offered considerable scope for widespread deportation. Heydrich was equally radical on mixed marriages. All Jewish partners of German spouses were destined for deportation. The only choice for the authorities would be between evacuation—that is, murder—and deportation to a so-called old-age ghetto. Half Jews who were married to Germans would be evacuated or deported to an old-age ghetto unless there were children who had been deemed second-degree *Mischlinge,* in which case the parent would be spared.[79]

The numbers at stake were small. There were fewer than twenty thousand mixed marriages in Germany.[80] According to Lösener, in 1939 there were sixty-four thousand first-degree and forty-three thousand second-degree *Mischlinge* in the Old Reich, Austria, and the Sudeten area.[81] True, there were many more non-German *Mischlinge* in other parts of Europe, but Heydrich probably had little fear that they would remain immune. After all, no one was worried about the morale of those married or related to Jews *outside* Germany; the argument that *Mischlinge* were half German also did not apply. So Heydrich's assault was not about numbers and all about asserting definitional power under the banner of a radical concept of race. The purpose of Wannsee was to reinforce the RSHA's preeminence in all aspects of the Jewish question.

SECURING COMPLIANCE AND COMPLICITY

A number of historians see Heydrich's actions as primarily a personal initiative designed to maintain or demonstrate his power.[82] Wolfgang Scheffler, for example, points out that Heydrich did not control the concentration camps and that thus a growing empire lay outside his jurisdiction. Wannsee was his attempt to reassert a declining position.[83] But when we bear in mind that Heydrich was now in charge of the Czech Protectorate, with a magnificent official residence in Prague, and that he had also been entrusted with masterminding an enormous deportation program, bringing him into contact with authorities all over Europe, it is hard to believe he was concerned about losing authority. By contrast, Eberhard Jäckel argues that Wannsee was a ceremonial event, designed to show that Heydrich had come out from Himmler's shadow, a view supported to some extent by Eichmann's postwar testimony. "The prime motive for Heydrich himself," Eichmann said in Jerusalem, "was doubtless to expand his power and authority." Elsewhere Eichmann spoke of Heydrich's "indulging his well-known vanity—that was his weakness, showing off a mandate which made him the master of Jews in all the areas occupied and influenced by Germany and thus demonstrating his enhanced influence."[84] Heydrich's choice of the stylish villa on the Wannsee lake adds to the sense that he was making a gesture.[85]

Yet the conference was not really about vanity. Instead, it was part of a concerted, coordinated campaign by Himmler and Heydrich to assert their supremacy. Heydrich's invitation, his opening remarks at the meeting, and indeed his follow-up letter to the participants, in which he expressed pleasure that "happily the basic line was established as regards the practical execution of the final solution of the Jewish question," all indicate that his major aims were to achieve unity and common purpose among the participants and above all to secure acceptance of the RSHA's leading role.[86] Two weeks before the invitations went out, both Himmler and Heydrich had held a series of meetings. On November 15, Himmler and Rosenberg had their lengthy confabulation on the "biological eradication" of European Jewry. Two days later, Himmler and Heydrich conferred to coordinate their policy on, among other things, "eliminating the Jews."[87] On November 24, it was Wilhelm Stuckart's turn to confer with Himmler. Number three of the four points in Himmler's calendar was "Jewish question— belongs to me."[88] If the postwar testimony of Bernhard Lösener is to be believed, Stuckart complained in the following weeks that Jewish matters were being taken away from the Ministry of the Interior. On November 28, Himmler had yet another meeting on the issue, this time conferring with the HSSPF of the Generalgouvernement, Friedrich-Wilhelm Krüger, to discuss the obstacles Governor Frank was putting in the way of "central management of Jewish questions."[89] Between the invitation and the conference there were more such encounters, most notably between Himmler and Bühler on January 13.

Himmler and Heydrich were thus making strenuous efforts to coordinate and centralize all initiatives on the Jewish question. Given the widespread support for anti-Jewish measures, we might wonder why this was necessary. The defense attorney for Eichmann in Jerusalem asked him whether Heydrich had any real reason to fear opposition. Eichmann's reply was instructive:

> According to the practice until then, all the offices were always trying, for departmental reasons, to delay things and make reservations—in other words, there was always a whole series of individual discussions in the long drawn-out deliberations held until then. Those were dragging on, and there was never a clear-cut solution achieved right away. This was the reason why Heydrich convened this Wannsee Conference, in order, as it were, to press through, on the highest level, his will and the will of the Reichsführer-SS and Chief of the German Police.[90]

Heydrich's real target was the civilian ministries—the other participants were brought in to strengthen his hand. In the weeks and months before the conference, Himmler and Heydrich had repeatedly clashed with the ministries over issues of competence. Both within Germany and in the occupied territories the demarcation lines were ill-defined. In autumn 1941, Heydrich's Security Police experienced regular run-ins with the Ministry for the Occupied Eastern Territories and particularly with the ministry's commissioners in the Baltic and White Russia. In early November, for example, Rudolf Lange, the head of *Einsatzkommando* 2 and regional chief for the Security Police in Riga, who attended the Wannsee Conference, had a number of angry exchanges with the Reich commissioner for the Ostland, Hinrich Lohse, about the imminent deportations to Riga.[91] In Poland the conflicts between Himmler's staff and the civilian administration were, if anything, even more intense. In May 1940 Governor Frank had stated unambiguously that the police were an enforcement arm of the government, though in practice he was never able to impose this view. A few days later, HSSPF Krüger complained to Himmler that the elevation of Frank's deputy, Josef Bühler, to *Staatssekretär* rank would mean that he, Krüger, would have to take orders from the younger Bühler. Krüger was duly promoted to *Staatssekretär* too.[92] In 1940–41 Frank was involved in a continual battle to prevent Heydrich from deporting Jews from the Reich to the Generalgouvernement.

Other ministries, too, particularly the Interior Ministry, had a fraught relationship with the RSHA. Nominally,

Himmler was subordinate to the minister of the interior. In practice, Minister Frick had abandoned any pretense of controlling Himmler; indeed, he had given up hope even of being informed as to what the RSHA was up to.[93] Yet some questions of prerogative remained, particularly the jealously guarded category of mixed-race Jews. Alone among the civilian representatives at Wannsee, probably only Martin Luther from the Foreign Office had resigned himself to subordination and had adapted by trying to be as helpful to the RSHA as possible.

It is perfectly possible that Himmler and Heydrich could have resolved demarcation issues on an individual basis with each agency. The series of November meetings suggests they were in the process of doing so. Yet, in the complicated power structure of the Third Reich, a collective acknowledgment among all the interested parties was of much greater worth in establishing power and precedents. Moreover, in the climate of a high-level meeting with a strong party and SS presence, the other ministerial representatives would be much more susceptible to group pressure.

There was yet another purpose to the meeting: Heydrich wanted to establish shared complicity. "The significant part from Heydrich's point of view," Eichmann claimed in Jerusalem, "was to nail down the Secretaries of State, to commit them most bindingly, to catch them by their words."[94] The events following the transport of Berlin Jews to Riga on November 29–30 had brought to a head the growing disquiet flowing back to Berlin from a variety of sources over the treatment of the German Jewish deportees, particularly after the first mass murders in Kovno and in Riga. The knowledge of these shootings soon made the rounds of the Berlin authorities; Bernhard Lösener claimed that in his case they represented a personal turning point. Both Heydrich and Himmler were undoubtedly concerned to enlist all agencies in their enterprise and prevent further murmurings. The last thing they wanted was for Hitler to worry about morale and once again rein in their activities. Moreover, with the first premonitions in December 1941 that Germany might not win the war, establishing common complicity was a powerful force to ensure that other agencies toed the line. Paradoxically, it would encourage them to hand over power to the RSHA to avoid taking on further responsibility. We know, for example, that Otto Bräutigam, who represented the Ministry for the Occupied Eastern Territories at one of the follow-up conferences to Wannsee, concluded in January that Germany could not win the war. At the follow-up conference in late January he ostentatiously displayed his willingness to make concessions to Heydrich's men. "As far as the Jewish question," he confided to one of his own colleagues, "he was quite happy to emphasize the responsibility of the SS and the police."[95]

Heydrich's aim of creating shared knowledge of murder explains one of the real oddities of the Wannsee protocol, namely its peculiar juxtaposition of euphemism and undisguised murderousness. On the one hand, the document is coy about killing and talks of "evacuation of Jews to the East." On the other hand, the language about eliminating Jewish workers is so open, and the implications for the rest so clear, as to render the euphemisms pointless as a disguise. The RSHA's natural tendency was to be extremely guarded. Euphemisms were its normal mode of communicating about murder and would have served here to remind the document's recipients of the codes they should use. At the same time it was so vital to ensure the participants' shared knowledge in the killing program that caution was abandoned. This was why Lammers, Stuckart, and others were at such pains after the war to deny having seen the protocol. How else to escape the trap that Heydrich had set them?

PARTICIPATING IN GENOCIDE

It was the "first time in my life," recalled Adolf Eichmann, that he had taken part "in such a conference in which . . . senior officials participated, such as Secretaries of State—it was conducted very quietly and with much courtesy, with much friendliness—politely and nicely, there was not much speaking and it did not last a long time, the waiters served cognac, and in this way it ended."[96] Even if not itself the deciding moment, then, Wannsee remains a powerfully symbolic one. These were not the barbarian hordes, pouring across the frontiers and slaughtering all that lay in their path. Here, in the refined atmosphere of an elegant villa, in a cultivated suburb, in one of Europe's most sophisticated capitals, fifteen educated, civilized bureaucrats from an educated, civilized society sat about, observing all due decorum. And here they gave the nod to genocide.

How could they have gone along with it? Did they believe in what they were doing? Or were they driven by secondary motives—competition for power perhaps or blind obedience to duty? Or were they merely weak, complying with a process over which they had no control?

The first point must be that a surprising number of clever men round the table were true believers, for whom racist nationalism was at the heart of their philosophy. The participants were by and large confirmed Nazis and not dutiful functionaries. The fact that so many of the senior men were so young was a sign that newcomers had managed to rise rapidly to positions of power. This was particularly true in the SS and party institutions, but in the government ministries, too, staunch Nazis had risen quickly up the ranks. New ministries such as Rosenberg's Ministry for the Occupied Eastern Territories and Goebbels's Propaganda Ministry (not represented at Wannsee), as well as the civilian administration in Poland, were stuffed full of party men; little remained of a civil service ethos. Alfred Meyer, for example, had joined the Nazi Party in 1928 and was a Nazi through and through—he had been gauleiter in Westphalia and a senior SA (Nazi paramilitary) man years before he entered

Rosenberg's ministry. His ministerial colleague Georg Leibbrandt had maintained contact with the party since 1930. In the Polish administration, Josef Bühler owed his position to his long-term personal contacts with Hans Frank—he had worked in Frank's legal practice in the 1920s.[97]

Even in the most established ministries, there had been ample opportunity for confirmed Nazis to advance rapidly. Indeed, of the participants at Wannsee, the one who could claim longest membership in the Nazi Party was from the Justice Ministry. Roland Freisler, a decorated First World War veteran, had joined the party in 1925. Before that he had a legal practice and served as a city deputy for the right-wing radical Völkisch-Sozialen Block. After 1925 he was the Nazis' legal adviser in Kassel, and in 1932 he became an outspoken Nazi deputy in the Prussian parliament. Within months of the Nazis' seizure of power, he was promoted up the Justice Ministry ladder to the position of *Staatssekretär*, first in Prussia, then in the Reich administration.[98] Wilhelm Stuckart was of a similar stamp. A fighter with the Freikorps in the civil war and a member of the radical right-wing student body the Skalden-Orden, he too, like Freisler, became a legal adviser to the Nazi Party in the 1920s. In the 1930s he quickly advanced to high rank in the SS. His fast-track promotion to departmental chief in the Interior Ministry in 1935 owed not a little to his party contacts. Stuckart personified a new generation of *Staatssekretär*—talented and highly qualified, capable of doing well under any circumstances, but ideologically committed to the Nazi Party.[99]

Some of the appointees were undoubtedly not up to the job. Rosenberg's staff was particularly notorious—Meyer was by general account "too weak to be good, too cowardly to sin," and Leibbrandt, whose previous experience had been as head of the Eastern Section in the Nazi Party Foreign Policy Office, was, like his boss, Rosenberg, a fanatic and not particularly competent.[100] But generally speaking, we need to abandon the stereotype of the neutral educated bureaucrat assiduously fulfilling orders handed down by ignorant, irrational Nazis. It remains one of the most striking characteristics of Wannsee that most of the best-educated participants were also long-standing Nazis. Of the eight men who had doctorates, six either were "old fighters" of the Nazi Party or had at least enjoyed close contacts with the party well before 1933.[101] The other two had long years of right-wing *völkisch*-national politics behind them: Rudolf Lange had belonged to the Burschenschaft Germania, while Gerhard Klopfer had been a member of the Deutscher Hochschulring.[102] These men's backgrounds provide powerful evidence of the substantial degree to which radical nationalist ideas had influenced Germany's educated youth even before 1933.

In some cases bonds of friendship and shared ideas linked the different institutions—the most striking instance being the ties between the SD's chief architect, Werner Best (not himself present at Wannsee), the party man Gerhard Klopfer, and the civil servant Wilhelm Stuckart. In autumn 1941 these men founded *Reich—Volksordnung—Lebensraum* (Reich—Ethnic Order—Living Space), a journal for an "ethnically based [*völkisch*] constitution and administration."[103] Men like Stuckart and Freisler were as deeply persuaded by Nazi ethnic-racial power politics as the party officials or the men in the RSHA. Though not a rabid antisemite, Freisler had published an article entitled "The Tasks of the Reich Justice System, Proceeding from a Biological Standpoint" in 1935.[104] The racial imperatives governing the state's activity emerged even more clearly in an essay he wrote a year later, "The Protection of Race and Racial Stock in the Emerging German Legal System," in which he argued that the racial mixing of the previous centuries had to be reversed.[105]

In short, ideas mattered at Wannsee. Yet when we look at the process by which these men edged toward genocide, it is clear that there was no simple transmutation of ideas into politics. For one thing, there were opportunists as well as ideologues present. Heydrich's chief henchman, Heinrich Müller, for example, had, before 1933, been a loyal servant of the Weimar state. It was his competence in the Munich police force that led Himmler and Heydrich to take him on to their staff, where he became a prime advocate of "preventive law enforcement," attacking the regime's enemies before they committed a crime.[106] In 1937, opposing Heydrich's (ultimately successful) efforts to promote "Gestapo Müller," the Munich deputy gauleiter recognized Müller's efforts combating the left:

> It must be acknowledged that he fought them extremely vigorously, at times flouting legal restrictions. But it is equally clear that had it been his allotted task to do so, Müller would have been equally vigorous against the right. With his enormous ambition and drive he would have gained the recognition of whatever superiors he was working for.[107]

At the heart of the RSHA and one of the most feared men in Germany, Müller was nevertheless one of the very last members round the Wannsee table to join the Nazi Party—he did so only in 1938.

Martin Luther had joined the Nazis a little before the seizure of power, in 1932, but was above all an entrepreneur or, as Walter Schellenberg of the RSHA put it, energetic but "governed solely by the calculation of the businessman."[108] With a successful business career behind him, he owed his rise in the Foreign Office mostly to the fact that he had become a general factotum for Joachim von Ribbentrop and his wife in the 1930s and had followed Ribbentrop into the office. When Luther entered the Foreign Office in 1938 he asked for jurisdiction over party affairs but requested that Jewish matters be left to another department. There is thus no basis for the historian Gerald Reitlinger's suggestion that Luther made "anti-semitism his life's work."[109] On the contrary, he took up Jewish matters only later, when it seemed the means to assure the Foreign Office some continued influence at a time when its scope for activity was waning.[110] The examples of Luther and Müller show us that opportunism, or a desire for order, or simply not questioning the validity of the tasks assigned could be sufficient reasons for participating in genocide.

More striking than opportunism, however, was how astonishingly far all the Wannsee participants, even those with a strong racial vision, had moved from where they had been even just a few years earlier. Wilhelm Stuckart's theoretical position on the Jews evolved markedly from the late 1930s to the early 1940s. Initially arguing that Jews were not inferior, only different, by 1942 he asserted that their lesser quality as human beings justified their extermination.[111] He may well have assumed in the 1930s that the Jewish problem would be solved by emigration.[112] In the 1930s Heydrich and Eichmann, too, had assumed, as revealed in position papers and memoranda dating from 1935 on, that the Jewish problem was primarily one of emigration. If we can trust the sources, even some leading members of the SD were taken aback by the violence of *Kristallnacht,* a pogrom they had not initiated.[113] Although the degree to which educated young men subscribed to Nazi ideas is noteworthy, the fact is that they nevertheless embarked on a journey that went far beyond anything they could have imagined.

Earlier chapters have suggested in general terms the forces that impelled them. At the center stood Hitler, setting the tone, prescribing the boundaries, licensing every radical action, and spanning a rhetorical canopy that could shelter the most brutal of actions. More than anything or anyone else, it was he who defined the pace and direction of the journey his men had traveled. It was his signals that had brought antisemitism to the top of the SD's agenda or that had prompted the Interior Ministry to chip away at Jewish citizenship rights for the better part of a decade.

In this evolving context, the Wannsee participants adapted and responded. Some of them played a major role in the process, others were more led than leading. Some were enthusiastic, others less so, their diverse responses reflecting both their dispositions and the pressures and opportunities associated with the particular offices they held. The advance guard at Wannsee was unquestionably formed by the men from the RSHA. All the civilian representatives felt under pressure from Himmler and Heydrich. Throughout the 1930s, as bureaucratic efficiency melded with radical ideology, Himmler and, beneath him, Heydrich had played increasingly central roles. They, more than any other figures, had insinuated radical ideology into the state apparatus. By keeping the concentration camps and the SS outside the state system, Himmler had posed a permanent threat to the bureaucracy and helped bring it into line.[114] After 1938, Heydrich became the pacesetter on the Jewish question. It was he who masterminded the forced emigration policy from Vienna and Berlin, he who superintended the deportations after the outbreak of war, he who drafted the increasingly murderous guidelines for the *Einsatzgruppen* in the Sudetenland, Poland, and Russia. His direct subordinate, Heinrich Müller, had a hand in almost every facet of Jewish persecution. Below Müller, Adolf Eichmann, the man who made the arrangements for the Wannsee Conference, would prove indefatigable as the orchestrator of deportations and the cajoler of Jewish administrations all across Europe, tricking and threatening them into cooperating with genocide.

Probably the least committed to the genocidal project, and the most reluctant to try to keep up with the RSHA's pace, was Friedrich Kritzinger. At fifty-one the oldest person present, he represented the shrinking group of bureaucrats who still embodied something of an earlier civil service ethos. Kritzinger and Erich Neumann from the Economics Ministry were the two civilian representatives at Wannsee who had joined the Nazi Party only after the Nazi seizure of power—in Kritzinger's case well after and clearly without enthusiasm. Neumann, a talented administrator with a successful career in the Prussian civil service behind him, joined both the party and the SS only in 1933; later, in 1942, he would leave public service and enter the business world. But

Neumann had been caught up in the atmosphere of the Four Year Plan organization and was the loyal servant of the extremely antisemitic Göring. By contrast, the Reich Chancellery, to which Kritzinger had been recruited in 1938 as a competent and approachable administrator, was one of the few ministries small and cohesive enough to have sustained something of its pre-Nazi values.[115]

Though not itself responsible for initiating measures, the Reich Chancellery had grown markedly in importance after 1938, above all because of the access to Hitler enjoyed by its chief, Heinrich Lammers (an advantage lost in 1943, when Martin Bormann blocked the gateway). Kritzinger, the number-two man in the ministry, was party to many administrative decisions that were illegal even by the judicial code then in force.[116] Yet there were a number of occasions on which he used his influence to slow down measures, particularly if they had implications for those Jews whom the department had identified as not beyond help—those in privileged mixed marriages and the *Mischlinge*. In 1940–41, for example, Kritzinger successfully opposed the Interior Ministry's proposal to declare German Jews stateless and thus "protectees" (*Schutzangehörige*) of the Reich, a proposal that would have facilitated their deportation. Kritzinger asserted at Nuremberg, with justice, that he had been no hardliner (*Scharfmacher*). "What incriminates him," writes the historian Hans Mommsen, "is less his occasional initiative than his weakness."[117] Even on the issue of the

Mischlinge, the Reich Chancellery eventually felt it had to yield ground to the radicals. It was Lammers who in autumn 1941 gave an approving nod to the idea of sterilizing all *Mischlinge*—at a time when the Interior Ministry was still resisting such measures.

Overall, the civilian ministries with domestic roles within Germany had no direct responsibility for killing. They made murder much easier, however, by moving with the tide and refining and consolidating the legal foundations for the expropriation and segregation of Germany's Jews. On April 20, 1940, to take just one of countless examples, Stuckart wrote to the Ministerial Council for Reich Defense on the treatment of Jewish forced labor under German labor law. Stuckart had noticed that Jews affected by work closures on New Year's Day, Easter Monday, Whit Monday, and Christmas Day were enjoying paid holidays. On his own initiative, Stuckart recommended the Jews be excluded from remuneration.[118] It was he who moved to have German Jews declared stateless, thus absolving the ministry of legal responsibility for deported Jews.[119] (This particular initiative was frustrated by Kritzinger in the Reich Chancellery and by Hitler's subsequent dictum that legislation on Jewish citizenship was irrelevant since after the war there would be no Jews in Germany.)[120] Yet even Stuckart, for all his intellectual kinship with Klopfer and Best, was still to some extent influenced by a moral climate different from that in Heydrich's RSHA.[121] Next to Kritzinger, he was probably the person who came to the Wannsee table with the most reservations, above all because of his ministry's attempts to protect half Jews and Jews in mixed marriages.

In the course of 1941 an increasing number of the participants had been in one way or another initiated into murder. The representatives of the Ministry for the Occupied Eastern Territories were well acquainted with it. In October they sent instructions to the commissioners in the field that there were no objections to eliminating Jews who could not work.[122] By mid-November they were arguing that economic considerations should not figure in the elimination of the "problem."[123] For his part, Josef Bühler, Hans Frank's deputy in the Generalgouvernement, could not fail to know a great deal about killing Jews. His civilian subordinates had set ration allocations and wages so low that Jews had either to obtain food illegally or die. In December, Bühler had been privy to Frank's speech calling for the Jews of the Generalgouvernement to be done away with one way or another.

Ministries and agencies that had no direct contact with the killing operations were also increasingly well informed. For one thing, the *Einsatzgruppen* in Russia produced regular detailed accounts about the numbers they had killed, and the distribution list for the summary reports was progressively expanded. We know that Martin Bormann in the Party Chancellery received copies, so his representative at Wannsee, Klopfer, would probably have seen them as well.[124] In October 1941 the Gestapo chief, Heinrich Müller, distributed the first five reports to the German Department in the Foreign Office. From the third one on, it was clear to the recipients that Jews were being killed quite separately from partisans. By the end of 1941 the mass murder of Soviet Jews was very widely known within the Foreign Office.[125] It is possible, but not certain, that in the winter of 1941 the Reich Chancellery also received these documents.[126] In the Interior Ministry, certainly, the facts were surfacing. Bernhard Lösener, Stuckart's deputy, described after the war hearing from another official the fate of the Berlin deportees to Riga.[127] Confronting Stuckart with this information (if Lösener's account is to be trusted), he was met with the reply, "Don't you know that these things are ordered at the highest level?"[128]

What is striking is how many people round the table had given direct killing orders or had themselves experienced killing. Heydrich's apparatus determined the rate of murder. The SS/SD leaders, Heydrich and Müller, directed the killing operations of the *Einsatzgruppen.* Heydrich may well have witnessed *Einsatzgruppen* killings at firsthand; he had certainly been in the field around the time of *Einsatzgruppen* murders and given orders for them to be intensified, as, for example, in Grodno at the end of June 1941.[129] We also know that his boss, Himmler, attended a mass shooting in August. In September or October 1941, according to his later testimony, Adolf Eichmann witnessed a mass shooting in Minsk.[130] Shortly before, Eichmann had called for the Jews of Serbia to be shot. The security chiefs in the General-gouvernement and the Riga district, Schöngarth and Lange, arrived at Wannsee dripping with blood. Lange had led *Einsatzkommando* 2 in Riga and been responsible for shooting the Riga Jews at the end of November 1941. Schöngarth had created the special *Einsatzgruppe* to carry out murders in the Galician territory. It was he who in November 1941 introduced the so-called *Schiessbefehl,* or shooting order, which called for Jews found outside the ghetto areas to be summarily shot.[131] In September 1941 Martin Luther of the Foreign Office approached Heydrich unsolicited, seeking his support for shooting Serbian Jews rather than deporting them.[132] His subordinate, Franz Rademacher, visited Serbia to determine conditions on the ground, where he found that the army was already solving the problem. Christopher Browning argues that it was Luther's energy and devotion to the cause that earned the Foreign Office a seat at the conference.[133] The oft-cited gap between the "desk murderers" and the men in the field barely applies at Wannsee.

It is thus small wonder that no one declined to attend the meeting on principle. No one arrived at Wannsee with even the faintest intention of speaking up for the Jews. In the pressured atmosphere, with such a strong corps of supporters from the RSHA, the SS, and the party, Heydrich was able to push forward with little opposition even on the contested

Mischling question. Only the borderline cases enjoyed any defense at all—the privilege of sterilization—and only Jews essential for German production were granted a temporary reprieve. No one raised objections to the proposals for murder. It was much too late for that.

A LARGELY SUCCESSFUL DAY

Did Heydrich get what he wanted at Wannsee? The protocol suggests the RSHA achieved two breakthroughs. First, the age-old conflict with the civilian authorities in the General-gouvernement over the Jewish question seemed to finally be resolved. Josef Bühler, according to the protocol, explicitly invited the RSHA to begin the Final Solution there. The foundations for this new accord had already been laid in December, when Hans Frank had met Hitler and gained an inkling of future plans, and in January, when Bühler met Himmler and left the meeting very satisfied. Whereas previously the RSHA had treated the Generalgouvernement as the "garbage dump" of the Reich, now it was promising to carry out ethnic cleansing. Removing Jews *from* the General-gouvernement, by whatever means, rather than dumping them *in* the region was something on which the RSHA and

Bühler could agree. In fact, disputes over who controlled what would continue, and Frank would suffer some decisive reversals in the course of the year. But all Bühler was interested in now was the speed with which the Security Police would be able to do away with the Jews.[1]

The RSHA's second breakthrough was even more striking. Wilhelm Stuckart of the Interior Ministry seemed to have buckled. It was predictable that Otto Hofmann, speaking for the SS Race and Settlement Office, should have echoed Heydrich's arguments about the *Mischlinge*. Less expected was Stuckart's response. Having anticipated an assault from Heydrich, his Jewish expert, Bernhard Lösener, had produced yet another paper, outlining the reasons why the *Mischlinge* should be protected.[2] But instead of holding the ministry's line, Stuckart now—according to the protocol—proposed the compulsory sterilization of *all Mischlinge*. His stance on mixed marriages was even more radical. Complaining about the administrative work involved in separating Jewish partners from their spouses, he called for a simple legislative act "such that the law in effect says: 'These marriages have been dissolved.'" Nothing now stood in the way of the deportation of the Jews.

Why did Stuckart give in? The most generous interpretation is that he was playing a clever game. At Nuremberg, he did not deny the position he had taken, but claimed that he had in fact been seeking to deflect the "evacuations": he knew all the while that widespread sterilization was not feasible.[3] According to Lösener and a former official in the Ministry of the Interior, Hans Globke, Stuckart had received information from his colleague Leonardo Conti that mass sterilization was not practicable during wartime (a fact that subsequent meetings indeed confirmed).[4] Stuckart claimed, said Lösener, that he was attempting delay tactics and hoped at the end of the war for a "noble gesture" from on high.[5] This is possible, but two points speak against it. The first is that the "compromise"—mass sterilization rather than the murder of the *Mischlinge*—had an established pedigree of which Stuckart would have been well aware.[6] In October 1941 Dr. Adolf Pokorny had proposed to Himmler that Soviet POWs be sterilized, thus making it "safe" to deploy them as workers on German soil.[7] In the same month, the chief of the Reich Chancellery, Heinrich Lammers, and the chief of the party's Racial Policy Office, Walter Gross, had had a conversation about the *Mischlinge,* after which Lammers said he would support the sterilization of all first-degree *Mischlinge.*[8] The second, even stronger argument against such a generous interpretation of Stuckart's conduct is his radical approach to mixed marriages. The proposal to dissolve them was never going to be postponed on feasibility grounds.

Whatever Stuckart's motives, the RSHA was certainly delighted. At several points in his Jerusalem testimony, Eichmann returned almost with glee to the "conversion" of State Secretary Stuckart. Questioned by his defense lawyer about the atmosphere among the participants, Eichmann said that "not only did everybody willingly indicate agreement, but there was something else, entirely unexpected, when they outdid and outbid each other, as regards the demand for a final solution to the Jewish question. The biggest surprise, as far as I remember, was not only Bühler but above all Stuckart, who was always cautious and hesitant but who suddenly behaved there with unaccustomed enthusiasm." Cross-examined by the judge about how openly murder was discussed at Wannsee, Eichmann said:

> Today, I no longer have any detailed recollection of this matter, Your Honor, but I know that these gentlemen stood together and sat together, and in very blunt words they referred to the matter, without putting it down in writing. I would definitely not be able to remember this, if I did not know that at that time I said to myself: Look at that . . . Stuckart, who was always considered to be a very precise and very particular stickler for the law, and here the whole tone and all the manner of speech were totally out of keeping with legal language. That is the only thing, I would say, which has actually remained imprinted on my mind.[9]

Heydrich's behavior at the end of the conference amply revealed his own satisfaction. In one of a series of interviews given in Argentina before his capture, Eichmann said:

I remember that at the end of this Wannsee Conference Heydrich, Müller and my humble self settled down comfortably by the fireplace and that then for the first time I saw Heydrich smoke a cigar or a cigarette, and I was thinking: Today Heydrich is smoking, something I have not seen before. And he drinks cognac—since I had not seen Heydrich take any alcoholic drink in years. . . . And after this Wannsee Conference we were sitting together peacefully, and not in order to talk shop, but in order to relax after the long hours of strain. I cannot say any more about this.[10]

In Jerusalem, Eichmann reaffirmed that Heydrich's "satisfaction was quite obvious" and that, despite his own insignificance, as he tried to claim, he had been asked to stay behind for "a glass or two or three of cognac."[11]

In some sense, Heydrich's pleasure was probably justified. Wannsee had underlined the RSHA's claim to mastery in the Jewish question. The Ministry of the Interior increasingly subordinated itself to Himmler's leadership even before Himmler replaced Wilhelm Frick as minister—and Stuckart became his *Staatssekretär*. But if Heydrich really believed that he had carried the day on the *Mischling* question, he was soon to be disappointed. It seems, even from the protocol itself, that he may have broached the issue quite tentatively since his remarks on the *Mischlinge* are described as "theoretical."[12] A note from the Ministry for the Occupied Eastern

Territories racial expert, Erhard Wetzel, suggested that the whole discussion had been only exploratory: "20th of the 1st, *Staatssekretär-Besprechung: Mischlinge* of the 1st degree *no* worse than hitherto. Question merely raised for discussion. General rejection also Führer Chancellery."[13]

True, there were early signs that Wannsee had indeed changed the climate when, on January 29, officials meeting in the Ministry for the Occupied Eastern Territories decided to treat Soviet *Mischlinge* as Jews.[14] But since these *Mischlinge* were half Russian (or half Lithuanian, and so on) rather than half German, the Ministry of the Interior's grounds for protecting the half Jews would scarcely have applied anyway. There was little evidence that half Jews had hitherto enjoyed much protection in Russia. In any case, Himmler subsequently rejected any formal guidelines on the matter outside Germany: "We only tie our hands with all these stupid definitions."[15] So the decision was rather an academic one.

More significant were two follow-up meetings to Wannsee that took place in March and October 1942, involving subordinates of the Wannsee participants.[16] At both meetings Eichmann and the party radicals sought agreement at the very least on Stuckart's compromise proposals but if possible on Heydrich's more extreme suggestions: evacuation of half Jews, evacuation or settlement in an old-age ghetto for Jews in mixed marriages. However, although the meetings passed radical suggestions up the line, on neither occasion did they come to anything. For one thing, mass sterilization did turn out to be impracticable, despite some indication in summer 1942 that X-ray treatment might be speedy and effective. For another, both the Ministry of Justice and the Ministry of Propaganda were worried about the implications of compulsory divorce. The former was worried about loss of jurisdiction, the latter about the implications for Catholic morale if the Vatican issued a blanket condemnation.[17] The Reich Chancellery also helped to slow down the proposals. But it was Hitler's unwillingness to tackle the matter in wartime that decided the matter.[18] Lammers said at Nuremberg that, after obtaining a lukewarm response from Hitler on the issue of the *Mischlinge* in March, the gentlemen in the Reich Chancellery "interpreted this moment as a definite victory over the RSHA." In October 1943 Justice Minister Otto Thierack and Himmler agreed not to deport *Mischlinge* for the duration of the war.[19]

As for mixed marriages, the October 1942 follow-up meeting did reaffirm the commitment to compulsory divorce. Here again, however, the initiative was blocked at a higher level, with Lammers interpreting Hitler's signals as meaning he did not wish to be bothered with such a proposal during the war.[20] Following a decree from Heinrich Müller of the Gestapo in December 1943, the regime began deporting formerly privileged Jewish widows after the deaths of their spouses. Starting in January 1945, some Jewish partners in existing marriages were also deported.[21] For the most part, though, the Jews in privileged mixed marriages were saved.

Wannsee had failed to provide the decisive breakthrough Heydrich had hoped for. Ultimately, the axiom proved true once again: when Hitler was hesitant, policy stagnated.

In relation to full and non-German Jews, there was no such hesitancy. The year 1942 was the most astounding year of murder in the Holocaust, one of the most astounding in the whole history of mankind. Up to March 1942, less than 10 percent of the Holocaust's eventual Jewish victims had died, predominantly in the Soviet Union and in Chelmno.[22] It had been the Soviet POW victims of German neglect, not Jews, whose deaths totaled in the millions. But the period from the beginning of killings at Belzec in mid-March 1942 through to mid-February 1943 saw the extermination of more than half of all the Jews who would die at the Nazis' hands.[23] How significant was the Wannsee Conference itself in unleashing this unbelievable tide?

Both Heydrich and Eichmann certainly talked up the meeting's significance at the time. Five days after Wannsee, Heydrich sent out a circular to all the regional Security Police chiefs, attaching Göring's July 1941 authorization of a plan for the "final solution" and assuring them that preparatory measures were now being implemented.[24] Toward the end of February, Heydrich sent out copies of the protocol, accompanying them with a note to the participants affirming that "happily the basic line" had now been "established as regards the practical execution of the final solution of the Jewish question."[25] In the aftermath of the conference, Eichmann spread word among his subordinates of the plan to exterminate European Jewry, as two of them, Dieter Wisliceny and Hermann Krumey, later testified.[26] In Jerusalem, too, Eichmann continued to underline Wannsee's significance:

> Well, it is quite easy to verify it, the Conference of Wannsee was very important, for here Heydrich received his authority as the person in charge of the solution, or the final solution of the Jewish question. From this point he regarded himself as having the authority in all these matters.[27]

There are signs that the protocol circulated among German officials throughout Europe. Thirty copies were produced; at a cautious estimate, each one reached five to ten officials.[28] We know that the officials in Minsk soon heard about the document, while on March 23, the Jewish expert in the German embassy in Paris, Carltheo Zeitschel, wrote to his superiors in the Foreign Office saying he had heard that a *Staatssekretär* meeting had taken place and asking for a copy of the minutes.[29]

The outcome of the conference galvanized Heydrich and Eichmann to new efforts. On January 31, 1942, Eichmann sent a circular to all the regional Gestapo centers concerning the new deportation program. At his trial, Eichmann pointed to this circular as the first direct consequence of the Wannsee meeting. This confirms that, at the very least, Wannsee opened the way to a massive new wave of deportations, as soon as the transport situation permitted.[30] The circular announced that whereas deportations had previously been constrained by the limited absorption facilities in the East, new possibilities for absorption were now being worked out—doubtless a coded reference to mass murder.[31] Transport difficulties prevented the onset of new deportations until March, when Eichmann was again very active, holding a series of meetings with Jewish advisers posted abroad, with junior officials from the Wannsee departments on the subject of sterilization, and with regional Gestapo leaders, making sure that they stuck to the Wannsee guidelines and did not "evacuate" elderly Jews who were supposed to go to Theresienstadt.[32]

At the conference Heydrich had made clear that he had yet to produce the overall plan required of him by Göring. Whether he ever submitted such a plan, we do not know. It has been argued that Goebbels refers to such a document in his diary entry of March 7: "I am reading a detailed paper from the SD and police on the final solution of the Jewish question. It raises a large number of issues. The Jewish Question must be solved now on a pan-European scale."[33] Heydrich's note accompanying the protocol made clear, however, that any final report could be completed only once the follow-up meeting to Wannsee (on March 6) had taken place.[34] Between the holding of that meeting on the sixth and Goebbels's entry on the seventh there was no time for the production and dissemination of such a comprehensive document. It seems likely, therefore, that Goebbels was referring to the Wannsee protocol itself, which he would have received just a few days before, and that it became the surrogate document of "closure."[35] The protocol was probably the closest the Nazis ever came to writing down their overall plan of genocide.

In the Generalgouvernement, preparations for the deportation of Lublin Jews to Belzec gathered momentum in late January.[36] Around this time Himmler and HSSPF Krüger carried out personnel changes among the SSPF in the Generalgouvernement. Only the really radical figures—Globocnik and Katzmann—remained in their posts. Those who did not seem radical enough were replaced.[37] From mid-February on, the surviving German Jews languishing in White Russia were murdered.[38] February 1942 also saw a significant expansion of plans for crematoria and gas chambers at Auschwitz. In March a new wave of deportations of German Jews began, this time to the Lublin area of Poland. At the same time, Slovakian Jews began to be dispatched to Auschwitz, where they would be worked to death rather than gassed. Lublin Jews were first murdered in Belzec in large numbers in the same month, while Sobibor claimed its first victims in April.[39]

This dismal narrative does not necessarily establish Wannsee itself as the decisive catalyst. For one thing, as we know, the killings at Belzec had been planned since the previous October; Auschwitz, too, had been set to begin operation since test killings the previous autumn, and transports would presumably have resumed without Wannsee. For another, historians such as Peter Longerich point out that German Jews sent in March 1942 to Piaski, Izbica, and Zamosc as well as to Warsaw were, like their predecessors in 1941, not killed straightaway but instead packed into the hovels of Polish Jews who had been sent on to the gas chambers. Longerich argues that as late as March 1942 the killings at Belzec still conformed to the "old" pattern of piecemeal "clearing operations" to make way for deportations, a pattern broken only in May–July 1942, when the killing program was greatly expanded. Some further decision must have taken place, Longerich insists, before the Nazi killings became truly comprehensive.[40]

Part of the problem here lies in what we consider a "decision." Himmler's direct and repeated involvement in widening the scope of killings in 1942 is well documented. The beginnings of mass murder through poison gas in the Generalgouvernement coincided with Himmler's visit to Krakow and Lublin on March 13–14, 1942. On April 17, 1942, a day after consulting with Hitler, Himmler personally ordered the killing of the Western European Jews in Lodz. His visit to Warsaw that day was also accompanied by a decision to construct a new extermination camp, Treblinka. Heydrich's assassination in early June served only to emphasize Himmler's leadership role and to add ferocity to his campaign. Following meetings with Hitler on July 14, Himmler launched a new, still more intense wave of killing. On July 18 he was in Auschwitz to inaugurate the real phase of mass gassings there. The following day he was in Lublin, from where he dispatched a telegram ordering HSSPF Krüger to kill all but a few Jews in the Generalgouvernement by the end of the year. Three days later, on July 22, the most intense phase of the Final Solution began with the deportations from Warsaw to Treblinka. The extermination of the last Jewish communities in the Ukraine began in May and June 1942, one of the few murder operations for which we have written orders from Himmler. Even after Wannsee, it seems, the process demonstrably did not function on its own and involved Himmler's continual interventions, on several occasions, it seems, after consultation with Hitler.[41]

In Jerusalem Eichmann, too, sought to refute the prosecutor's suggestion that after Wannsee the operation ran like clockwork:

ACCUSED [EICHMANN]: That is wrong, Mr. Attorney General. Each individual wave had to be ordered afresh. The documents show this also. And once such orders had been issued, if I was competent to act and received orders from my superior, the entire matter of trains, for example, also had to be dealt with. That is correct. As for the camps in the East, or the absorption stations, they were named—how they . . .

PRESIDING JUDGE: The question is directed to the physical possibilities of extermination—that is how I understand the question, and that would appear to depend on two factors—as mentioned by the Attorney General—transport possibilities and absorption possibilities. Is that correct?

ACCUSED: In principle that is correct, Your Honor, but first the orders had to be issued.

ATTORNEY GENERAL: But an order already existed—there was this order—this order by the Führer from summer of 1941, and you saw this document, signed by Göring.[42]

ACCUSED: In that case for all practical purposes, after the Wannsee Conference Heydrich, for example, would have had to say to me: "Well, Eichmann, everything is settled, approved, see to it now, do what you want, but the matter must be settled one-two-three."

But that is not how things were: Himmler kept issuing orders, time and time again he issued orders. All the many hundreds of offices that were somehow involved had to carry out their part, and I was also unfortunately caught up in this. As a result of these measures I had to deal with the matters on which I received orders—I have never denied this and am not denying it, either. I cannot deny it, because that is what happened.[43]

This was not just Eichmann hiding behind orders; Himmler really had been continually involved. And yet developments in 1942 show an obvious difference from the situation in autumn 1941. In September and October 1941, transports were dispatched without a clear idea of what would happen to them, and to areas where there was no clear policy of what was to happen. Regional officials felt their way and did some of the center's thinking for it, though always in close liaison with Berlin. Once transports resumed in March 1942, all such tentativeness was gone. No one was sent to a region where their ultimate fate was uncertain. German Jews were sent to the Lublin region, where extermination camps were in place and where it was understood that first the Polish Jews and then they would be murdered. There was no indeterminate eastern territory still under discussion. Above all, though, the whole operation was now being planned from Berlin.

Decisions still had to be made. Throughout 1942, for example, there would be a fluctuating balance between manpower needs and the project of genocide. Given the likelihood that Germany would lose the war and thus be unable to complete its genocidal program, Himmler's interventions and the shifting pressures for or against retaining Jewish manpower were to be of vital significance in determining which remnant of European Jewry might survive. But the decisions were not about whether to kill or not, simply about when and in what order to kill. In this respect, the Wannsee protocol captured a decisive transition in German policy, a transition from murderous deportations to a clear program of murder.

Wannsee itself was not the moment of decision. Nobody at Wannsee, not even Heydrich, was senior enough to decide on such matters. As the fate of the *Mischlinge* revealed, if the right arguments could be passed up to Hitler, agreements sealed at the Wannsee Conference could be undone. Conversely, where Hitler's approval was assured, Himmler would undoubtedly have proceeded even if Heydrich had not secured the active and passive assents he obtained at Wannsee. The Wannsee protocol was rather a signpost indicating that genocide had become official policy. Yet Heydrich undoubtedly took the assent he had engineered at Wannsee very seriously. The signals he and Eichmann gave out after the event showed it had immeasurably strengthened their confidence. In May, Heydrich visited security officials in France for the last time before his assassination; his account of the planning for the Final Solution emphasized the agreements reached on January 20.[44] Speaking to one another with great politeness, sipping their cognac, the *Staatssekretäre* really had cleared the way for genocide.

APPENDIX:

THE PROTOCOL

This translation is a revised version of the translation in *The Wannsee Protocol and a 1944 Report on Auschwitz by the Office of Strategic Services,* vol. II of *The Holocaust: Selected Documents in Eighteen Volumes,* ed. John Mendelsohn (New York: Garland, 1982), with stylistic clarifications by Dan Rogers and Mark Roseman.

Stamp: Top Secret

30 copies

16th copy

Minutes of discussion.

I.

The following persons took part in the discussion about the final solution of the Jewish question that took place in Berlin, 56-58 Am Grossen Wannsee, on January 20, 1942.

Gauleiter Dr. Meyer and Reichsamtleiter Dr. Leibbrandt	Reich Ministry for the Occupied Eastern Territories
Staatssekretär Dr. Stuckart	Reich Ministry of the Interior
Staatssekretär Neumann	Plenipotentiary for the Four Year Plan
Staatssekretär Dr. Freisler	Reich Ministry of Justice
Staatssekretär Dr. Bühler	Office of the Generalgouvernement
Unterstaatssekretär Dr. Luther	Foreign Office
SS-Oberführer Klopfer	Party Chancellery
Ministerialdirektor Kritzinger	Reich Chancellery
SS-Gruppenführer Hofmann	Main Office for Race and Settlement
SS-Gruppenführer Müller SS-Obersturmbannführer Eichmann	Reich Main Security Office
SS-Oberführer Dr. Schöngarth, Chief of the Security Police and the SD in the Generalgouvernement	Security Police and SD
SS-Sturmbannführer Dr. Lange, Commander of the Security Police and the SD for the General District of Latvia, deputy of the Chief of the Security Police and the SD for the Reich Commissariat Ostland	Security Police and SD

II.

At the beginning of the discussion, Chief of the Security Police and the SD, SS-Obergruppenführer Heydrich reported that the Reich marshal had delegated to him the preparations for the final solution of the Jewish question in Europe and that this discussion had been called for the purpose of clarifying fundamental questions. The wish of the Reich marshal to have a draft sent to him concerning organizational, policy, and technical prerequisites for the final solution of the European Jewish question makes it necessary to ensure in advance that the central organizations involved be brought together and their policies properly coordinated.

Overall control of the final solution of the Jewish question lies, irrespective of geographical boundaries, with the Reichsführer-SS and chief of the German police (chief of the Security Police and the SD).

The chief of the Security Police and the SD then gave a short report of the struggle that had been carried on thus far against this enemy, the essential points being the following:

a) the expulsion of the Jews from every sphere of life of the German people,
b) the expulsion of the Jews from the living space of the German people.

In pursuit of these ends, the only provisional solution available had been a planned acceleration of Jewish emigration out of Reich territory.

By order of the Reich marshal, a Reich Central Office for Jewish Emigration was created in January 1939, under the leadership of the chief of the Security Police and the SD. Its most important tasks were

a) to make all necessary arrangements for the preparation for an increased emigration of the Jews,
b) to direct the flow of emigration,
c) to speed the procedure of emigration in each individual case.

The aim of all this was to cleanse German living space of Jews in a legal manner. The drawbacks of such enforced accelerated emigration were clear to all involved. In the absence of any alternative, however, these drawbacks had initially to be accepted.

In the ensuing period, the tasks associated with emigration became not just a German problem but one confronting the authorities of the countries to which the flow of emigrants was directed. Financial difficulties, such as the demand by various foreign governments for increasing sums of money to be presented at the time of the landing, the lack of shipping space, increasing restriction of entry permits, or the canceling of such, radically increased the difficulties of emigration. In spite of these difficulties, 537,000 Jews were sent out of the country between the takeover of power and the deadline of October 31, 1941. Of these,

approximately 360,000 were in Germany proper on January 30, 1933,
approximately 147,000 were in Austria (Ostmark) on March 15, 1938,

approximately 30,000 were in the Protectorate of Bohemia and Moravia on March 15, 1939.

The Jews themselves, or their political organizations, financed the emigration. In order to avoid impoverished Jews remaining behind, the principle was followed that wealthy Jews had to finance the emigration of poor Jews; this was arranged by imposing a suitable tax, that is, an emigration tax, which was used for financial arrangements in connection with the emigration of poor Jews and was imposed according to wealth.

Apart from the necessary Reichsmark exchange, foreign currency had to be presented at the time of landing. In order to prevent a drain of German foreign exchange holdings, the foreign Jewish financial organizations were—with the help of Jewish organizations in Germany—made responsible for arranging an adequate amount of foreign currency. Up to October 30, 1941, these foreign Jews donated a total of around $9,500,000.

In the meantime the Reichsführer-SS and chief of the German police had prohibited emigration of Jews due to the dangers of emigration in wartime and the possibilities of the East.

III.

Instead of emigration, the new solution has emerged, after prior approval by the Führer, of evacuating Jews to the East.

These actions are nevertheless to be seen only as temporary

relief but they are providing the practical experience that is of great significance for the coming final solution of the Jewish question.

Approximately eleven million Jews will be involved in the final solution of the European Jewish question, distributed as follows among the individual countries:

COUNTRY	NUMBER
A.	
Germany proper	131,800
Austria	43,700
Eastern territories	420,000
Generalgouvernement	2,284,000
Bialystok	400,000
Protectorate of Bohemia and Moravia	74,200
Estonia	free of Jews
Latvia	3,500
Lithuania	34,000
Belgium	43,000
Denmark	5,600
France/occupied territory	165,000
unoccupied territory	700,000
Greece	69,600
Netherlands	160,800
Norway	1,300

Appendix: The Protocol

B.

Bulgaria	48,000
England	330,000
Finland	2,300
Ireland	4,000
Italy, including Sardinia	58,000
Albania	200
Croatia	40,000
Portugal	3,000
Romania, including Bessarabia	342,000
Sweden	8,000
Switzerland	18,000
Serbia	10,000
Slovakia	88,000
Spain	6,000
Turkey (European portion)	55,500
Hungary	742,800
USSR	5,000,000
Ukraine	2,994,684
White Russia, excluding Bialystok	446,484

Total	over 11,000,000

The number of Jews given here for foreign countries includes, however, only those Jews who still adhere to the Jewish faith, since some countries still do not have a definition of

163

the term *Jew* according to racial principles. Dealing with the problem in these individual countries will meet with difficulties due to the attitude and outlook of the people there, especially in Hungary and Romania. Thus, for example, even today the Jew can buy documents in Romania that will officially prove his foreign citizenship.

The influence of the Jews in all walks of life in the USSR is well known. Approximately five million Jews live in the European part of the USSR, in the Asian part scarcely a quarter of a million.

The breakdown of Jews residing in the European part of the USSR by occupation was approximately as follows:

Agriculture 9.1 %
Urban workers 14.8 %
In trade 20.0 %
Employed by the state 23.4 %
In private occupations such as medical profession, press,
   theater, etc. 32.7%

In the course of the final solution and under appropriate leadership, the Jews should be put to work in the East. In large, single-sex labor columns, Jews fit to work will work their way eastward constructing roads. Doubtless the large majority will be eliminated by natural causes. Any final remnant that survives will doubtless consist of the most resistant elements. They will have to be dealt with appropriately because otherwise, by natural selection, they would form the germ cell of a new Jewish revival. (See the experience of history.)

In the course of the practical execution of the final solution, Europe will be combed from west to east. Germany proper, including the Protectorate of Bohemia and Moravia, will have to be dealt with first due to the housing problem and additional social and political necessities.

The evacuated Jews will first be sent, in stages, to so-called transit ghettos, from where they will be transported to the East.

SS-Obergruppenführer Heydrich went on to say that an important prerequisite for the evacuation as such is the exact definition of the persons involved.

It is intended not to evacuate Jews over sixty-five years old but to send them to an old-age ghetto—Theresienstadt is being considered for this purpose.

In addition to these age groups—of the approximately 280,000 Jews in Germany proper and Austria on October 31, 1941, approximately 30 percent are over sixty-five years old—severely wounded veterans and Jews with war decorations (Iron Cross I) will be accepted in the old-age ghettos. With this expedient solution, in one fell swoop many interventions will be prevented.

The larger evacuation actions would commence when the military situation allowed. Regarding the handling of the final solution in those European countries occupied and influenced by us, it was proposed that the appropriate experts of the Foreign Office discuss the matter with the relevant official of the Security Police and SD.

In Slovakia and Croatia the matter is no longer so difficult, since the most substantial problems in this respect have already been brought near a solution. In Romania the government has in the meantime also appointed a commissioner for Jewish affairs. In order to settle the question in Hungary, it will soon be necessary to force an adviser for Jewish questions onto the Hungarian government.

With regard to taking up preparations for dealing with the problem in Italy, SS-Obergruppenführer Heydrich considers it opportune to contact the chief of police with a view to these problems.

In occupied and unoccupied France, the registration of Jews for evacuation will in all probability proceed without great difficulty.

Unterstaatssekretär Luther calls attention in this matter to the fact that in some countries, such as the Scandinavian states, difficulties will arise if this problem is dealt with thoroughly and that it will therefore be advisable to defer actions in these countries. In view of the small numbers of Jews affected, this deferral will in any case not cause any substantial limitation.

The Foreign Office sees no great difficulties for Southeast and Western Europe.

SS-Gruppenführer Hofmann plans to send an expert to

Hungary from the Main Office for Race and Settlement for general orientation at such time as the chief of the Security Police and the SD takes up the matter there. It was decided to assign this expert from the Main Office for Race and Settlement, who will not work actively as an assistant to the police attaché.

IV.

In the planning of the final solution, the Nuremberg Laws will in effect provide the general framework, though a prerequisite for reaching an overall solution is finding an answer to the question of mixed marriages and persons of mixed blood.

The chief of the Security Police and the SD discusses the following points, at first theoretically, in regard to a letter from the chief of the Reich chancellery:

1) Treatment of Persons of Mixed Blood of the First Degree

Persons of mixed blood of the first degree will, as regards the final solution of the Jewish question, be treated as Jews.

From this treatment the following exceptions will be made:

a) Persons of mixed blood of the first degree married to persons of German blood if their marriage has resulted in children (persons of mixed blood of the second degree). These persons of mixed blood of the second degree are to be treated essentially as Germans.

b) Persons of mixed blood of the first degree, for whom the highest offices of the party and state have already issued exemption permits in any sphere of life.

Each individual case must be examined, and it is not ruled out that the decision may be made to the detriment of the person of mixed blood.

The prerequisite for any exemption must always be the personal merit of the person of mixed blood (not the merit of the parent or spouse of German blood).

Persons of mixed blood of the first degree who are exempted from evacuation will be sterilized in order to prevent any offspring and to eliminate the problem of persons of mixed blood once and for all. Such sterilization will be voluntary. But it is the precondition for remaining in the Reich. The sterilized "person of mixed blood" is thereafter free of all restrictions to which he was previously subjected.

2) Treatment of Persons of Mixed Blood of the Second Degree

Persons of mixed blood of the second degree will be treated essentially as persons of German blood, with the exception of the following cases, in which the persons of mixed blood of the second degree will be considered as Jews:

a) The person of mixed blood of the second degree was born of a bastard marriage (both parents persons of mixed blood).
b) The person of mixed blood of the second degree has a racially especially undesirable appearance that marks him outwardly as a Jew.
c) The person of mixed blood of the second degree has a particularly bad police and political record that shows that he feels and behaves like a Jew.

In these cases, however, exceptions should not be made if the person of mixed blood of the second degree has married a person of German blood.

3) Marriages between Full Jews and Persons of German Blood

Here it must be decided case by case whether the Jewish partner should be evacuated or, in view of the effects of such a step on the German relatives of the marriage, sent to an old-age ghetto.

4) Marriages between Persons of Mixed Blood of the First Degree and Persons of German Blood

a) Without children

   If no children have resulted from the marriage, the person of mixed blood of the first degree will be evacuated or sent to an old-age ghetto (same treatment as in the case of marriages between full Jews and persons of German blood, point 3).

b) With children

   If children have resulted from the marriage (persons of mixed blood of the second degree), they will, if they are to be treated as Jews, be evacuated or sent to a ghetto along with the parent of mixed blood of the first degree. If these children are to be treated as Germans (regular cases), they are exempted from evacuation, as is therefore the parent of mixed blood of the first degree.

5) Marriages between Persons of Mixed Blood of the First Degree and Persons of Mixed Blood of the First Degree or Jews

   In these marriages all members of the family (including the children) will be treated as Jews and therefore be evacuated or sent to an old-age ghetto.

6) Marriages between Persons of Mixed Blood of the First Degree and Persons of Mixed Blood of the Second Degree

   In these marriages both partners will be evacuated or sent to an old-age ghetto without consideration of whether the marriage has produced children, since possible children will as a rule have stronger Jewish blood than the Jewish person of mixed blood of the second degree.

SS-Gruppenführer Hofmann is of the view that extensive use should be made of sterilization, particularly as the *Mischling,* presented with the choice of evacuation, would rather submit to sterilization.

State Secretary Dr. Stuckart points out that the practical implementation of the strategies outlined for dealing with the mixed race and mixed marriage questions will entail endless administrative work. In order, on the other hand, to ensure that the biological facts are fully taken into account, State Secretary Dr. Stuckart proposes proceeding to forced sterilization.

Furthermore, to simplify the problem of mixed marriages, possibilities must be considered, such that the law in effect says: "These marriages have been dissolved."

With regard to the question of the effect of the evacuation of Jews on the economy, State Secretary Neumann stated that, as long as replacements were not available, Jews employed in industries vital to the war effort could not be evacuated.

SS-Obergruppenführer Heydrich pointed out that, according to the rules he had approved for carrying out the evacuations, these Jews would not be evacuated anyway.

State Secretary Dr. Bühler stated that the Generalgouvernement would welcome it if the final solution of this problem could begin in the Generalgouvernement, since on the one hand transportation does not play such a large role there nor would the question of labor supply hamper this action. The Jews must be removed from the territory of the Generalgouvernement as quickly as possible because of the particular danger there of epidemics being brought on by Jews. Jewish black-market activities were persistently destabilizing the region's economy. The 2½ million Jews in the region were in any case largely unable to work.

State Secretary Dr. Bühler stated further that the solution to the Jewish question in the Generalgouvernement is the responsibility of the chief of the Security Police and the SD and that his efforts would be supported by the officials of the Generalgouvernement. He had only one request—that the Jewish question be solved as quickly as possible.

In conclusion, the various possible kinds of solution were discussed, with both Gauleiter Dr. Meyer and State Secretary Dr. Bühler taking the position that certain preparatory activities for the final solution should be carried out immediately in the territories in question, without alarming the populace.

With a final request from the chief of the Security Police and the SD that the participants provide him with necessary cooperation and assistance in carrying out his tasks, the meeting was closed.

NOTES

1. "PERHAPS THE MOST SHAMEFUL DOCUMENT"

1. The international war crimes trials ended in 1946. The United States then prosecuted second-rank officials, also at Nuremberg. The "Ministries Case" involved the civil servants at Wannsee (among others). See *The Ministries Case, Trials of War Criminals before the Nuernberg Military Tribunals under Control Council Law No. 10*, vols. 13–15, Nuremberg, Oct. 1946–Apr. 1949.

2. My translation from Robert M. W. Kempner, *Ankläger einer Epoche: Lebenserinnerungen* (Frankfurt/Main: Ullstein, 1983), p. 311. Brigadier General Telford Taylor had replaced Robert Jackson as chief American prosecutor.

3. John A. S. Grenville, "Die 'Endlösung' und die 'Judenmischlinge' im Dritten Reich," *Das Unrechtsregime: Internationale Forschung über den Nationalsozialismus,* ed. Ursula Büttner with Werner Johe and Angelika Voss (Hamburg: Christians, 1986), p. 108.

4. Kempner, *Ankläger,* pp. 310–12; Leni Yahil, "Himmler's Timetable," *Yad Vashem Studies* 28 (2000): 352.

5. Eberhard Jäckel, "On the Purpose of the Wannsee Conference," *Perspectives on the Holocaust: Essays in Honor of Raul*

Hilberg, ed. James S. Pacy and Alan P. Wertheimer (Boulder: Westview Press, 1995), p. 39.

6. On the protocol's authenticity, see Wolfgang Scheffler, "Die Wannsee-Konferenz und ihre historische Bedeutung," *Erin-nern für die Zukunft* (Berlin: Gedenkstätte Haus der Wannsee-Konferenz, n.d. [1992]), pp. 30–31.

7. The best summary is Eberhard Jäckel and Jürgen Rohwer, *Der Mord an den Juden im Zweiten Weltkrieg* (Stuttgart: Deutsche Verlags-Anstalt, 1985).

8. Precisely for this reason, surveys of these debates usually list the same few names—Lucy Davidowicz and Gerald Fleming on the one hand, Martin Broszat and Hans Mommsen on the other.

9. For the clearest and most carefully argued syntheses along these lines, see Christopher R. Browning, *Fateful Months: Essays on the Emergence of the Final Solution* (New York: Holmes and Meier, 1985); Browning, *The Path to Genocide: Essays on Launching the Final Solution* (Cambridge: Cambridge University Press, 1992); Philippe Burrin, *Hitler and the Jews: The Genesis of the Holocaust* (London: Edward Arnold, 1994).

10. Raul Hilberg, *The Destruction of the European Jews,* rev. and def. ed. (New York: Holmes and Meier, 1985); Hans Mommsen, "The Realization of the Unthinkable: The 'Final Solution of the Jewish Question' in the Third Reich," *From Weimar to Auschwitz: Essays in German History* (Oxford: Basil Blackwell, 1991), pp. 224–53; Martin Broszat, "Hitler und die 'End-lösung': Aus Anlass der Thesen von David Irving," *Viertel-jahrshefte für Zeitgeschichte,* 25 (1977): 739–75.

11. Daniel Goldhagen seeks to explain the motivation of perpe-trators at the lower level. See his *Hitler's Willing Executioners: Ordinary Germans and the Holocaust* (New York: Knopf, 1996).

12. Saul Friedländer, *Nazi Germany and the Jews: The Years of Perse-cution, 1933–1939* (London: Phoenix Giant, 1997); Ian Ker-shaw, *Hitler, 1889–1936: Hubris,* and *Hitler, 1936–1945: Nemesis* (Harmondsworth: Penguin, 2000).

Notes

13. Ulrich Herbert, *Best: Biographische Studien über Radikalismus, Weltanschauung und Vernunft, 1903–1989* (Bonn: J. H. W. Dietz Verlag, 1996); Peter Longerich, *Politik der Vernichtung: Eine Gesamtdarstellung der nationalsozialistischen Judenverfolgung* (Munich: Piper Verlag, 1998).
14. Some of the best of this recent work is summarized in Ulrich Herbert, ed., *National Socialist Extermination Policy* (Oxford: Berghahn Books, 1999).

2. *MEIN KAMPF* TO MASS MURDER, 1919–41

1. Burrin, *Hitler and the Jews,* p. 26, citing Hitler in a conversation in 1923.
2. Hitler's comments in the Leipzig newspaper *Der Nationalsozialist,* reproduced in Eberhard Jäckel, *Hitler's World View: A Blueprint for Power* (Cambridge: Harvard University Press, 1981), p. 57.
3. Jäckel, *Hitler's World View,* p. 58.
4. Quoted in John Lukacs, *The Hitler of History* (New York: Vintage, 1997), p. 182.
5. Richard J. Evans, *Lying about Hitler: History, Holocaust, and the David Irving Trial* (New York: Basic Books, 2001), pp. 72–73.
6. Max Domarus, ed., *Hitler: Speeches and Proclamations, 1935–1938* (London: I. B. Tauris, 1992), p. 758.
7. Oded Heilbronner, "The Place of Anti-Semitism in Modern German History," *Leo Baeck Institute Year Book,* vol. 20 (1990), p. 571.
8. See Hermann Graml, "Zur Genesis der Endlösung," *Das Unrechtsregime: Internationale Forschung über den Nationalsozialismus,* ed. Ursula Büttner, vol. 2: *Verfolung—Exil—Belasteter Neubeginn* (Hamburg: Christians Verlag, 1986), pp. 2–18.
9. Hans-Günther Adler, *Der verwaltete Mensch: Studien zur Deportation der Juden aus Deutschland* (Tübingen: J. C. B. Mohr/Paul Siebeck, 1974), pp. xxv–xxvi.
10. Hitler in a letter to Adolf Gemlich; quoted in Friedländer, *Nazi Germany,* p. 72.

11. Longerich, *Politik der Vernichtung*, pp. 25–30.
12. Hans Mommsen, "Realization," p. 230.
13. Günther Deschner, *Reinhard Heydrich: Statthalter der totalen Macht* (Esslingen am Neckar: Bechtle Verlag, 1977), p. 184.
14. The reference here is to Karl A. Schleunes's classic *The Twisted Road to Auschwitz: Nazi Policy toward German Jews, 1933–1939* (Urbana: University of Illinois Press, 1970).
15. Mommsen, "Realization," p. 227.
16. This view is encouraged by Bernhard Lösener, "Dokumentation: Das Reichsministerium des Innern und die Judengesetzgebung," *Vierteljahrshefte für Zeitgeschichte* 19 (1961): 262–312.
17. Mommsen, "Realization," p. 233; Uwe Dietrich Adam, *Judenpolitik im Dritten Reich* (Düsseldorf: Droste Verlag, 1972), pp. 206–07.
18. Friedländer, *Nazi Germany*, pp. 146–47.
19. Quoted in Kershaw, *Nemesis*, p. 1.
20. Friedländer, *Nazi Germany*, p. 181.
21. See the discussion in Evans, *Lying about Hitler*, pp. 52–62.
22. Quoted in Richard Breitman, *The Architect of Genocide: Himmler and the Final Solution* (New York: Knopf, 1991), p. 54.
23. Raul Hilberg, *Perpetrators, Victims, Bystanders: The Jewish Catastrophe, 1933–1945* (London: HarperCollins, 1992), pp. 21–24.
24. Michael Wildt, ed., *Die Judenpolitik des SD, 1935 bis 1938: Eine Dokumentation* (Munich: R. Oldenbourg Verlag, 1995), pp. 40–45, 100–05; Claudia Steur, *Theodor Dannecker: Ein Funktionär der "Endlösung"* (Essen: Klartext Verlag, 1997), p. 25; Longerich, *Politik der Vernichtung*, p. 210; Deschner, *Reinhard Heydrich*, p. 166.
25. See Detlev Grieswelle, "Hitlers Rhetorik in der Weimarer Zeit" (Diss., University of Saarbrück 1969); Friedländer, *Nazi Germany*, p. 102.
26. Longerich, *Politik der Vernichtung*, pp. 25–30.
27. Cited in Hans-Heinrich Wilhelm, *Die Einsatzgruppe A der Sicherheitspolizei und des SD, 1941/1942* (Frankfurt/Main: Peter Lang, 1996), pp. 15–16, n. 9.
28. See Bernd Weisbrod, "The Crisis of Bourgeois Society in

Notes

Interwar Germany," *Fascist Italy and Nazi Germany: Comparisons and Contrasts,* ed. Richard Bessel (Cambridge: Cambridge University Press, 1996), p. 36, and Bernd Weisbrod, "Violence and Sacrifice: Imagining the Nation in Weimar Germany," *The Third Reich between Vision and Reality: New Perspectives on German History, 1918–1945,* ed. Hans Mommsen (Oxford: Berg, 2001), pp. 5–21.

29. Ulrich Herbert, "Vernichtungspolitik: Neue Antworten und Fragen zur Geschichte des 'Holocaust,'" *Nationalsozialistische Vernichtungspolitik, 1939–1945: Neve Forschungen und Kontroversen* (Frankfurt/Main: Fischer, 1998), p. 41.

30. Herbert, *Best,* pp. 42–68.

31. Ulrich Herbert, "Ideological Legitimization and Political Practice of the Leadership of the National Socialist Secret Police," Mommsen, *Third Reich,* pp. 95–108.

32. Herbert, "Ideological Legitimization," p. 95; Deschner, *Reinhard Heydrich,* p. 83.

33. Heydrich's biographer Günther Deschner himself falls prey to this image of the value-free technocrat.

34. Herbert, *Best,* pp. 88–100.

35. See the remarks about Theodor Dannecker's background in Steur, *Dannecker;* see also Deschner, *Reinhard Heydrich,* pp. 160 and 166.

36. Michael Burleigh, *The Third Reich: A New History* (London: Macmillan, 2000), p. 189.

37. Adler, *Verwaltete Mensch,* p. 3.

38. Christopher Browning, *The Final Solution and the German Foreign Office: A Study of Referat DIII of Abteilung Deutschland, 1940–1943* (New York: Holmes and Meier, 1978), pp. 12–17; Wildt, *Die Judenpolitik des SD,* pp. 40–45, 100–05.

39. Avraham Barkai, *From Boycott to Annihilation: The Economic Struggle of German Jews, 1933–1943* (Hanover: University Press of New England, 1989).

40. Graml, "Zur Genesis," p. 6.

41. Burrin, *Hitler and the Jews,* p. 60.

42. Helmut Krausnick and Hans-Heinrich Wilhelm, *Die Truppe*

Notes

*des Weltanschauungskrieges: Die Einsatzgruppen der Sicherheits-
polizei und des SD, 1938–1942* (Stuttgart: Deutsche Verlags-
Anstalt, 1981), p. 623.

43. *Judenkenner,* Oct. 27, 1935; quoted in Adler, *Verwaltete Mensch,*
p. 60.

44. Cited in Burrin, *Hitler and the Jews,* p. 62.

45. Mommsen, "Realization," p. 233.

46. Henry Friedlander, *The Origins of Nazi Genocide: From Euthanasia to the Final Solution* (Chapel Hill: University of North Car-
olina Press, 1995), p. 39.

47. Friedländer, *Nazi Germany,* p. 312. See also Heydrich's speech
in Breitman, *Architect,* p. 59.

48. Hitler was surprised that the Polish issue led to European war,
and even in early September he was prepared to negotiate with
the Poles. See Martin Broszat, *Nationalsozialistische Polenpolitik,
1939–1945* (Stuttgart: Deutsche Verlags-Anstalt, 1961), p. 10.

49. Tens of thousands of Jews were brutally driven across the
demarcation line with the Soviet Union, sometimes only to
find themselves forced back by the Soviets. An agreement
with the USSR put a stop to these measures in December
1939. On the evidence that the intentions at this stage were
not genocidal, see Krausnick and Wilhelm, *Truppe,* pp. 71,
107; Hans Safrian, *Die Eichmann-Männer* (Vienna: Europa Verlag, 1993), pp. 71–72.

50. Safrian, *Eichmann-Männer,* pp. 72ff.; Dieter Pohl, *Von der
"Judenpolitik" zum Judenmord: Der Distrikt Lublin des General-
gouvernements, 1939–1944* (Frankfurt am Main: Peter Lang,
1993), pp. 54–55.

51. Twenty-eight hundred Gypsies had been deported as well. See
Ralf Ogorreck, *Die Einsatzgruppen und die "Genesis der Endlösung"* (Berlin: Metropol Verlag, 1996), p. 172.

52. Burrin, *Hitler and the Jews,* p. 77; Adler, *Verwaltete Mensch,* p. 72.

53. The historian Richard Breitman is among the most distinguished of those who believe that Hitler and Himmler were in
fact committed to genocide from the beginning of 1941. See

the discussion on p. 54 and p. 182, n. 6. There is no room here to respond to all the arguments, but see the account in Longerich, *Politik der Vernichtung,* pp. 273–92.

54. Safrian, *Eichmann-Männer,* p. 88.
55. Pohl, *"Judenpolitik,"* pp. 54–55.
56. Safrian, *Eichmann-Männer,* pp. 68, 79ff., 90.
57. Longerich, *Politik der Vernichtung,* p. 243.
58. Jürgen Förster, "The Relation between Operation Barbarossa as an Ideological War of Extermination and the Final Solution," *The Final Solution: Origins and Implementation,* ed. David Cesarani (London: Routledge, 1994), p. 87; Dieter Pohl, "Die Ermordung der Juden im Generalgouvernement," Herbert, *Nationalsozialistische Vernichtungspolitik,* p. 99.
59. Friedlander, *Origins,* pp. 62, 86ff., 136–37, 272; Götz Aly, "'Judenumsiedlung': Überlegungen zur politischen Vorgeschichte des Holocaust," Herbert, *Nationalsozialistische Vernichtungspolitik,* p. 86.
59a. German original in Longerich, *Politik der Vernichtung,* p. 243.
60. Pohl, *"Judenpolitik,"* pp. 26ff.; Krausnick and Wilhelm, *Truppe,* pp. 80–87; Förster, "Operation Barbarossa," pp. 88–89.
61. Breitman, *Architect,* p. 139.
62. Susanne Heim and Götz Aly, "The Holocaust and Population Policy: Remarks on the Decision on the 'Final Solution,'" *Yad Vashem Studies* 24 (1994): 58.
63. Safrian, *Eichmann-Männer,* p. 79.
64. Safrian, *Eichmann-Männer,* pp. 71, 97, 106.
65. Quoted in Jeremy Noakes and Geoffrey Pridham, eds., *Nazism, 1919–1945,* vol. 3 (Exeter: University of Exeter Press, 1995), p. 1094.
66. Burrin, *Hitler and the Jews,* p. 95.
67. At various times, Generals Manstein, Guderian, Hoth, Küchler, and Reichenau all endorsed the struggle against the Jewish subhumans. See Wilhelm, *Einsatzgruppe A,* pp. 15–16, n. 9.
68. Reprinted in Yitzhak Arad, Yisrael Gutman, and Abraham Margaliot, eds., *Documents on the Holocaust* (Lincoln: University

of Nebraska Press, 1999), p. 376. See also Krausnick and Wilhelm, *Truppe,* p. 136.

69. Walter Manoschek, *"Serbien ist judenfrei": Militärische Besatzungspolitik und Judenvernichtung in Serbien, 1941/42* (Munich: R. Oldenbourg Verlag, 1993), p. 191.

70. See Förster, "Operation Barbarossa"; Christian Gerlach, *Kalkulierte Morde: Die deutsche Wirtschafts- und Vernichtungspolitik in Weissrussland, 1941 bis 1944* (Hamburg: Hamburger Edition, 1999); Christoph Dieckmann, "Der Krieg und die Ermordung der Litauischen Juden," Herbert, *Nationalsozialistische Vernichtungspolitik,* pp. 292–329.

71. Longerich, *Politik der Vernichtung,* p. 298, quoting Herbert Backe.

72. Götz Aly, *"Final Solution": Nazi Population Policy and the Murder of the European Jews* (London: Arnold, 1995), p. 201. In 1939 continental Europe required imports of twelve to thirteen million tons of grain a year. Those numbers were bound to increase in wartime because of loss of efficiency.

73. Christian Streit, *Keine Kameraden: Die Wehrmacht und die Sowjetischen Kriegsgefangenen* (Stuttgart: Deutsche Verlags-Anstalt, 1978), p. 142ff.; Dieckmann, "Der Krieg," p. 318.

74. Arad, Gutman, and Margaliot, *Documents on the Holocaust,* p. 378.

75. Echoing the work of Alfred Streim, Ralf Ogorreck believes that the stress on cooperating with the military meant there would not have been secret instructions in the early weeks (*Einsatzgruppen,* pp. 95–109). Helmut Krausnick believes that the actions that followed showed that the verbal orders must have exceeded written instructions (Krausnick and Wilhelm, *Truppe,* p. 161). Christian Gerlach, too, believes that some kind of exterminatory intention must have been voiced in premeetings at Pretzsch or in Berlin (*Kalkulierte Morde,* pp. 629–30). In similar vein, see Breitman, *Architect,* p. 164. We know, for example, that Heydrich distinguished between short-term and final goals, but it is not clear whether the final goal was to deport the purged remainder farther east—this

would fit in with the European deportation plans he had been making since the spring—or to kill the remainder. See the Introduction in Peter Witte et al., eds., *Der Dienstkalender Heinrich Himmlers 1941/1942* (Hamburg: Christians Verlag, 1999), p. 70.

76. Longerich, *Politik der Vernichtung,* pp. 321–52.
77. Christian Gerlach, "Die Einsatzgruppe B 1941/2," *Die Einsatzgruppen in der besetzten Sowjetunion 1941/2,* ed. Peter Klein, (Berlin: Edition Hentrich, 1997), pp. 57–58.
78. Ogorreck, *Einsatzgruppen,* pp. 95–109.
79. The October 1941 report from *Einsatzgruppe* A suggests that from the start "the goal of the cleansing operation of the Security Police, in accordance with the fundamental orders, was the most comprehensive elimination of the Jews possible" (Breitman, *Architect,* p. 169). See also the discussion of the response of Franz Stahlecker, head of *Einsatzgruppe* A, to Reichskommisar Hinrich Lohse's new directives in Browning, *Path to Genocide,* pp. 109–10. Browning's interpretation, that Stahlecker's proposals to create single-sex ghettos were a cover for murder, seems to me more plausible than Longerich's more literal interpretation (see Longerich, *Politik der Vernichtung,* pp. 394–95).
80. Christian Streit, "Wehrmacht, Einsatzgruppen, Soviet POWs, and Anti-Bolshevism in the Emergence of the Final Solution," Cesarani, *Final Solution,* p. 106.
81. Gerlach, *Kalkulierte Morde,* p. 573.
82. Kershaw, *Hitler, 1936–1945,* p. 469.
83. Dieckmann, "Der Krieg," pp. 316–19; Gerlach, *Kalkulierte Morde,* p. 636.
84. Browning, *Path to Genocide,* pp. 105–06; Kershaw, *Hitler, 1936–1945,* p. 469; Witte et al., *Dienstkalender,* p. 185, n. 15.
85. Longerich, *Politik der Vernichtung,* pp. 362–69; Ogorreck, *Einsatzgruppen,* pp. 179–81; Gerlach, *Kalkulierte Morde,* pp. 566ff., 648; Gerlach, "Einsatzgruppe B," pp. 57–58.
86. Witte et al., *Dienstkalender,* p. 71.

Notes

3. MASS MURDER TO GENOCIDE

1. Czeslaw Madajczyk, "Hitler's Direct Influence on Decisions Affecting Jews during World War II," *Yad Vashem Studies* 20 (1990): 53–68.
2. Cited in Evans, *Lying about Hitler*, p. 78.
3. Breitman, *Architect*, pp. 159ff.; Gerlach, *Kalkulierte Morde*, pp. 648–49.
4. Quoted in translation in Arad, Gutman, and Margaliot, *Documents on the Holocaust*, p. 233.
5. Aly, "'Judenumsiedlung,'" p. 91; Aly, *"Final Solution,"* pp. 171–72.
6. Longerich, *Politik der Vernichtung*, p. 288. It is known that from the end of 1940 or the beginning of 1941, preparations were being made for large-scale deportations of all Jews under German influence to some eastern area. Was Hitler still thinking of creating a special territory or did he really have murder in mind? The latter interpretation is possible. Hitler's military adjutant, Gerhard Engel, who after the war published a diary of his experiences using undated notes he had taken while in Hitler's service, recorded a comment of Hitler's that he retrospectively dated to February 1941. Asked about the Madagascar plan, which no longer looked feasible, Hitler said that "he now had some other—not exactly more friendly— things in mind." Cited in Hilberg, *Destruction*, vol. 2, p. 399. Most contemporary evidence suggests, however, that in spring 1941 the thinking was about deportations to the Soviet Union.
7. Longerich, *Politik der Vernichtung*, p. 422.
8. Safrian, *Eichmann-Männer*, pp. 108ff.
9. Karin Orth, "Rudolf Höss und die 'Endlösung der Judenfrage': Drei Argumente gegen die Datierung auf den Sommer 1941," *Werkstatt Geschichte* 18 (1997): 45–58.
10. Orth, "Rudolf Höss," p. 52.
11. Longerich, *Politik der Vernichtung*, p. 424.
12. Kershaw, *Hitler, 1936–1945*, p. 462.

13. Longerich, *Politik der Vernichtung,* p. 427
14. Burrin, *Hitler and the Jews,* p. 101; Pohl, *"Judenpolitik,"* p. 87.
15. Kershaw, *Hitler, 1936–1945,* p. 476.
16. Pohl, *Von der Judenpolitik,* pp. 91–92.
17. Peter Witte, "Two Decisions concerning the 'Final Solution to the Jewish Question': Deportations to Lodz and Mass Murder in Chelmno," *Holocaust and Genocide Studies* 9 (1995): 319, 323–34; Kershaw, *Hitler, 1936–1945,* pp 472–75.
18. Longerich, *Politik der Vernichtung,* p. 438; Witte, "Two Decisions," pp. 321–25; Kershaw, *Hitler, 1936–1945,* p. 479.
19. Christian Gerlach, "The Wannsee Conference, the Fate of German Jews, and Hitler's Decision in Principle to Exterminate all European Jews," *The Holocaust: Origins, Implementation, Aftermath,* ed. Omer Bartov (London: Routledge, 2000), p. 110.
20. Christian Gerlach, "Die Ausweitung der deutschen Massenmorde in den besetzten sowjetischen Gebieten im Herbst 1941: Überlegungen zur Vernichtungspolitik gegen Juden und sowjetische Kriegsgefangene," *Krieg, Ernährung, Völkermord: Deutsche Vernichtungspolitik im Zweiten Weltkrieg* (Zurich: Pendo Verlag, 2001), p. 72.
21. Stalin had announced the decisions at the end of August. See Longerich, *Politik der Vernichtung,* pp. 429–30.
22. See Witte, "Two Decisions," pp. 321–26; Steur, *Theodor Dannecker,* pp. 63–65; Longerich, *Politik der Vernichtung,* p. 430; Kershaw, *Hitler, 1936–1945,* p. 478.
23. See esp. Burrin, *Hitler and the Jews.*
24. Manoschek, *"Serbien ist Judenfrei,"* pp. 185–87; Pohl, *"Judenpolitik,"* p. 94; Gerlach, *Kalkulierte Morde,* pp. 646–51; Longerich, *Politik der Vernichtung,* p. 443; Witte, "Two Decisions," p. 322. It is possible that the orders to build the camp at Sobibor were also given at this time and that exploratory moves were being made to construct a gas camp in eastern Galicia near Lvov (Thomas Sandkühler, *"Endlösung" in Galizien: Der Judenmord in Ostpolen und die Rettungsinitiativen von Bertold Beitz, 1941–1944* [Bonn: J. H. W. Dietz Nachfolger, 1996]).

There is some dispute about the Auschwitz date. See Franciszek Piper, "Gas Chambers and Crematoria," *Anatomy of the Auschwitz Death Camp*, ed. Yisrael Gutman and Michael Berenbaum (Bloomington: Indiana University Press, 1994), pp. 157 and 176, n. 6, but also Jean-Claude Pressac, "The Machinery of Mass Murder at Auschwitz," Gutman, *Anatomy*, p. 242, n. 62, and Karin Orth, *Das System der nationalsozialistischen Konzentrationslager: Eine politische Organisationsgeschichte* (Hamburg: Hamburger Edition, 1999), p. 139. Orth shows the links between the gassings and the euthanasia and Soviet POW actions in "Rudolf Höss," pp. 49–51.

25. Wolfgang Scheffler, "Chelmno, Sobibor, Belzec und Majdanek," Jäckel and Rohwer, *Der Mord*, p. 148.

26. Koeppen's information was indirect and it is very possible that it dated back to before the deportation decision and that the deportation itself was the "reprisal." It is possible, too, that Hitler still held back with an eye to Roosevelt, even though he was losing faith in the chances of averting America's entry into the war (Lukacs, *Hitler of History*, p. 192; Longerich, *Politik der Vernichtung*, p. 431).

27. Kershaw, *Hitler, 1936–1945*, p. 479.

28. On Hitler's perception of the military situation, see Browning, *Path to Genocide*, pp. 112–17.

29. Aly, *"Final Solution,"* p. 231.

30. Gerlach, *Kalkulierte Morde*, p. 618–19.

31. Manoschek, *"Serbien ist Judenfrei,"* pp. 185–90.

32. Manoschek, *"Serbien ist Judenfrei,"* p. 188.

33. Witte et al., *Dienstkalender*, p. 66; Gerlach, *Kalkulierte Morde*, p. 186; Dieter Pohl, *Nationalsozialistische Judenverfolgung in Ostgalizien, 1941–1944: Organisation und Durchführung eines staatlichen Massenverbrechens* (Munich: Oldenbourg, 1996), pp. 140ff.; Sandkühler, *"Endlösung" in Galizien*, pp. 138–40; Longerich, *Politik der Vernichtung*, p. 455.

34. Witte et al., *Dienstkalender*, pp. 201–02; Pohl, *Nationalsozialistische Judenverfolgung*, pp. 140–43; Sandkühler, *"Endlösung" in Galizien*, pp. 151–52, 407.

Notes

35. On Himmler and gas, see Breitman, *Architect*, p. 160ff. On July 16, 1941, the police authorities in the Warthegau requested the extermination of Jews unable to work (Madajczyk, "Hitler's Direct Influence," p. 56, n. 12). In Latvia there were rumors in early August that the Germans intended to gas Jewish women there. See Gerlach, *Kalkulierte Morde*, pp. 648–49.
36. Raul Hilberg, *Documents of Destruction: Germany and Jewry, 1933–1945* (London: W. H. Allen, 1972), p. 87.
37. Cited in Burrin, *Hitler and the Jews*, p. 119.
38. Ian Kershaw, "Improvised Genocide? The Emergence of the 'Final Solution' in the Warthegau," *Transactions of the Royal Historical Society*, 6th series (1992): 51–78; Deborah Dwork and Robert Jan van Pelt, *Auschwitz: 1270 to the Present* (New York: Norton, 1996), p. 294.
39. Bogdan Musial, *Deutsche Zivilverwaltung und Judenverfolgung im Generalgouvernement* (Wiesbaden: Harrassowitz, 1999), p. 195.
40. Sandkühler, *"Endlösung" in Galizien*, pp. 138–40.
41. Pohl, *"Judenpolitik,"* pp. 99–100; Witte et al., *Dienstkalender*, p. 233 and n. 35; Sandkühler, *"Endlösung" in Galizien*, p. 136; Bogdan Musial, "The Origins of 'Operation Reinhard': The Decision-Making Process for the Mass Murder of the Jews in the Generalgouvernement," *Yad Vashem Studies* 28 (2000): 116–18.
42. Pohl, *"Judenpolitik,"* pp. 105–06; Aly, *"Final Solution,"* p. 232; Musial, "Origins," p. 145.
43. See Hitler's comments conveyed by Martin Bormann to Heinrich Lammers, head of the Reich Chancellery, in Krausnick and Wilhelm, *Truppe*, p. 627.
44. See Evans, *Lying about Hitler*, p. 88.
45. Adler, *Verwaltete Mensch*, p. 62.
46. Kershaw, *Hitler, 1936–1945*, p. 484.
47. See Heydrich's statement in Hans-Günther Adler, *Theresienstadt 1941–1945. Das Antlitz einer Zwangsgemeinschaft: Geschichte, Soziologie, Psychologie* (Tübingen: J. C. B. Mohr/Paul Siebeck, 1955), pp. 720–22.

48. Heydrich said that Arthur Nebe and Emil Otto Rasch (the commanders of *Einsatzgruppen* B and C, respectively) could take Jews into the "camps for communist prisoners in the operation area" (Burrin, *Hitler and the Jews*, p. 128).

49. Gerlach, *Kalkulierte Morde*, p. 650.

50. Adler, *Theresienstadt*, pp. 720–22; see also Sandkühler, *"Endlösung" in Galizien*, p. 135.

51. The document is cited in Gerald Fleming, *Hitler and the Final Solution* (Oxford: Oxford University Press, 1986), pp. 70–71.

52. See Adam, *Judenpolitik*, p. 309, citing Serge Lang and Ernst von Schenck, *Portrait eines Menschheitsverbrechers: Nach den hinterlassenen Memoiren des ehemaligen Reichsministers Alfred Rosenberg* (St. Gallen: Zollikofer, 1947), p. 129, and the discussions in Christopher Browning, *Nazi Policy, Jewish Workers, German Killers* (Cambridge: Cambridge University Press, 2000), pp. 48–49, and Witte et al., *Dienstkalender*, p. 262, n. 46.

53. Cited in Adler, *Verwaltete Mensch*, p. 63.

54. Kershaw, *Hitler, 1936–1945*, p. 485, citing Goebbels's diary.

55. Werner Jochmann, ed., *Adolf Hitler: Monologe im Führer-Hauptquartier, 1941–1944* (Hamburg: Albrecht Kanus Verlag, 1980), p. 30–31; see also the discussion in Evans, *Lying about Hitler*, p. 72. The odd comment about the Jewish state came at a time when Hitler was attempting to make contact with Arab leaders.

56. Kershaw, *Hitler, 1936–1945*, p. 488.

57. Kershaw, *Hitler, 1936–1945*, p. 478.

58. Shlomo Aronson, "Hitlers Judenpolitik, die Alliierten und die Juden," *Vierteljahrshefte für Zeitgeschichte* 32 (1984): 51–52.

59. Fleming, *Hitler and the Final Solution*, p. 104.

60. This point seems to me the weakness of Christian Gerlach's otherwise pertinent questions about Hitler's statement to the Grand Mufti. See Gerlach's *Krieg, Ernährung, Völkermord*, p. 147, n. 240.

61. Longerich, *Politik der Vernichtung*, pp. 434, 449; Gerlach, *Kalkulierte Morde*, p. 751.

62. For David Irving, this telephone message proves Hitler's opposition to the murders of the Jews as a whole! See Irving, *Hitler's War*, p. 505.
63. English translation in Richard Breitman, *Official Secrets: What the Nazis Planned. What the British and Americans Knew* (London: Penguin, 1998), p. 82.
64. Breitman, *Official Secrets*, p. 82, drawing on the testimonies collected in Fleming, *Hitler and the Final Solution.*
65. Goebbels's diary entry for November 22, 1941, cited in Evans, *Lying about Hitler*, p. 76.
66. Lösener, "Dokumentation," p. 310.

4. THE MEETING

1. Deschner, *Reinhard Heydrich;* Shlomo Aronson, *Reinhard Heydrich und die Frühgeschichte von Gestapo und SD* (Stuttgart: Deutsche Verlags-Anstalt, 1971); Herbert, *Best.*
2. Kurt Pätzold and Erika Schwarz, *Tagesordnung: Judenmord. Die Wannsee-Konferenz am 20. Januar 1942* (Berlin: Metropol, 1992), p. 89.
3. Peter Klein, *Die Wannsee-Konferenz vom 20. Januar 1942: Analyse und Dokumentation* (Berlin: Hentrich, 1995), p. 31.
4. Penciled notation makes clear that the address was changed. The prosecutor at Nuremberg, Robert M. W. Kempner, claimed (wrongly) to have identified Eichmann's handwriting. See Kempner, *Eichmann und Komplizien* (Zürich: Europa Verlag, 1961), p. 129. In fact the address changes were inserted by the recipients after a phone call. We do not know whether the first address was given in error or whether Heydrich changed his mind and sought a new venue (Klein, *Wannsee-Konferenz*, p. 8).
5. See the list of invitees in the invitations to Martin Luther and Alfred Meyer, reproduced in Pätzold and Schwarz, *Tagesordnung*, pp. 88–90.
6. Following the convention in existing translations, *Staatssekretär*

has been rendered here as "state secretary." In normal English usage "secretaries of state" are, of course, ministers, which these men were definitely not. They were, however, political appointments and in that sense closer to the undersecretary of state.

7. Robert Kempner, *Das Dritte Reich im Kreuzverhör: Aus den Unveröffentlichten Vernehmungsprotokollen des Anklägers* (Königstein/Taunus: Athenäum/Droste Taschenbücher, 1980), p. 189. Kempner was interrogating Erich Neumann.

8. See, e.g., Martin Gilbert, *Holocaust Journey* (New York: Columbia University Press, 1999), p. 43.

9. There are some odd omissions, however, notably representatives of the Führer Chancellery and the army.

10. We can surmise that the addition was made before November 28 because a memorandum from Adolf Eichmann notes that, following Friedrich-Wilhelm Krüger's visit on the twenty-eighth, it was decided to revise the list slightly. Memorandum reproduced in Pätzold and Schwarz, *Tagesordnung*, p. 90.

11. There is some uncertainty about who exactly was to be invited. There is a memo from Eichmann to the effect that Hans Frank's deputy, Josef Bühler, and HSSPF Krüger were to be added to the list. The list of invitees to be found in the invitations sent out on November 29, however, includes Bühler's boss, Hans Frank (and not Bühler), as well as Krüger. In the list of invitees to be found in the note sent to Krüger a couple of days later, on December 1, Bühler is back on the list, rather than Frank. The wording of the draft note to Krüger suggests also that Krüger himself was not invited in the end. See the invitations reproduced in Pätzold and Schwarz, *Tagesordnung*, p. 89–90, and, above all, Klein, *Wannsee-Konferenz*, pp. 29–30. See also Gerlach, "Wannsee Conference," p. 116, and n. 35, below.

12. We do not know exactly when Heydrich ordered his subordinates to attend. It is possible that Rudolf Lange from the Soviet Union was a late addition.

13. Lösener, "Dokumentation," p. 297.

14. Gerlach, "Wannsee Conference," p. 119; Beate Meyer, *"Jüdische Mischlinge," Rassenpolitik und Verfolgungserfahrung, 1933–1945* (Hamburg: Dölling und Galitz Verlag, 1999), pp. 90ff.

15. See the memo "Wünsche und Ideen des Auswärtigen Amtes zu der vorgesehenen Gesamtlösung der Judenfrage in Europa" drawn up by Referat DIII for Martin Luther, December 8, 1941, reproduced in Pätzold and Schwarz, *Tagesordnung,* p. 91.

16. In "The Wannsee Conference Reconsidered Fifty Years After: SS Strategy and Racial Politics in the Third Reich," *Remembrance and Recollection: Essays on the Centennial Year of Martin Niemöller and Reinhold Niebuhr and the Fiftieth Year of the Wannsee Conference,* ed. Hubert Locke and Marcia Littell (Lanham, Md.: University Press of America, 1996), p. 60, Henry R. Huttenbach suggests that we know that Heydrich agreed at this stage to put Foreign Office matters on the agenda. I think this idea is based on a misunderstanding of an ambiguous reference to "his subordinates" (meaning Luther's, not Heydrich's) in Breitman, *Architect,* pp. 224–25. Raul Hilberg proposes that Heinrich Lammers, the well-informed minister in charge of the Reich Chancellery, believed that the proceedings were of broader significance still, telling his subordinates to watch for forthcoming invitations from the RSHA to make sure they attended as a "listening post." This comment, I think, however, is based on Lammers's rather muddled testimony from 1946. His later testimony makes clear that this particular instruction followed rather than preceded Wannsee and was meant to imply that the Reich Chancellery should play a very limited role. See Lammers's testimony of April 8, 1946, reproduced in Pätzold and Schwarz, *Tagesordnung,* p. 133; his later testimony, in *Trials of War Criminals,* vol. 13, p. 414; and Dieter Rebentisch, *Führerstaat und Verwaltung im zweiten Weltkrieg: Verfassungsentwicklung und Verwaltungspolitik, 1939–1945* (Stuttgart: Franz Steiner Verlag, 1989), pp. 434ff.

17. We deduce that they telephoned because we know that until the eighth the participants still believed the meeting would go ahead. On that day Luther's subordinate Franz Rademacher

presented him with notes "for tomorrow's meeting" (Safrian, *Eichmann-Männer,* p. 169). Since the cancellation does not appear in the otherwise complete Foreign Office records of the meeting, word of it probably came by phone.

18. Officials in the Interior Ministry believed that it was the forthcoming Reichstag session that originally led to Wannsee's postponement. See the Ministry for the Occupied Eastern Territories memo reproduced in Klein, *Wannsee-Konferenz,* p. 40.

19. My translation of Goebbels's entry for December 13, 1941, quoted in Gerlach, *Krieg, Ernährung, Völkermord,* p. 114.

20. This is a reference to the forthcoming Wannsee meeting. The text of Frank's speech was known at the time of the war crimes trial of 1945–46 and was in fact the first hint to the Allies of the existence of the meeting. Frank's speech quoted in Gerlach, *Krieg, Ernährung, Völkermord,* p. 122.

21. My translation from Gerlach, *Krieg, Ernährung, Völkermord,* p. 112.

22. My translation from Jochmann, *Adolf Hitler,* p. 229.

23. My translation from Jochmann, *Adolf Hitler,* p. 263.

24. This point is well made by Kershaw, *Hitler, 1936–1945,* p. 487.

25. Gerlach argues that the "decision" must be about the Jews rather than about the declaration of war since there was no logical reason the onset of hostilities with the United States would have prevented Rosenberg from discussing anti-Jewish measures.

26. See Gerlach, "Wannsee Conference," p. 150, n. 109, and Browning, *Nazi Policy,* p. 54, n. 78.

27. Klein, *Wannsee-Konferenz,* p. 38.

28. Kershaw, *Hitler, 1936–1945,* pp. 450–57.

29. "Die Villenkolonien in Berlin-Wannsee, 1870–1945," *Villenkolonien in Wannsee, 1870–1945: Grossbürgerliche Lebenswelt und Ort der Wannsee-Konferenz* (Berlin: Hentrich, 2000), pp. 14–69; Norbert Kampe, "Zur Ausstellung im Garten der Gedenk-

stätte," *Villenkolonien,* pp. 8–13; Gideon Botsch, "Der SD in Berlin-Wannsee, 1937–1945: Wannsee-Institut, Institut für Staatsforschung und Gästehaus der Sicherheitspolizei und des SD," *Villenkolonien,* pp. 70–95.

30. Contrary to speculation, Minoux did not finance Hitler.

31. Johannes Tuchel, *Am grossen Wannsee 56-58: Von der Villa Minoux zum Haus der Wannsee-Konferenz* (Berlin: Hentrich, 1992), pp. 38, 76, 96.

32. Tuchel, *Am grossen Wannsee,* pp. 105–08.

33. Fifteen would include Heydrich but not the stenotypist and Rolf Günther, Eichmann's deputy.

34. Hilberg, *Destruction,* vol. 2, p. 421.

35. In terms of rank, Krüger, not Schöngarth, was the appropriate counterpart to Bühler. Yet the wording of the (draft) note to Krüger suggests that he was never invited. Peter Klein speculates that Schöngarth was invited as the more politic guest, given the well-known and long-standing animosity between Krüger and Frank/Bühler (*Die Wannsee-Konferenz,* pp. 13–14; see also Hilberg, *Perpetrators,* p. 48). Another virtue of Schöngarth, from Heydrich's point of view, was that in the complicated SS and Security Police structure Schöngarth, though Krüger's subordinate, was also answerable to Heydrich, unlike Krüger, who, as HSSPF, was directly answerable to Himmler. See also n. 11, above.

36. "Das Protokoll dieser Konferenz war lang, obgleich ich das Unwesentliche nicht einmal hatte stenographieren lassen," Adolf Eichmann, "Götzen," unpublished ms., Haifa, 1961, p. 226. On Günther, see p. 219.

37. *Trials of War Criminals,* vol. 13, p. 414.

38. See the note from Rosenberg's racial expert, Erhard Wetzel, on the *Mischlinge* discussion, which suggests it was exploratory only (Götz Aly and Susanne Heim, *Vordenker der Vernichtung: Auschwitz und die deutschen Pläne für eine neue europäische Ordnung* [Hamburg: Hoffmann and Campe, 1991]), p. 470. See also my discussion later in this chapter, pp. 114ff.

39. The original of the protocol can be found in the Politisches Archiv des Auswärtigen Amtes, Berlin, Ref Inland IIg/177/165–180. The best facsimile is in Peter Klein, *Die Wannsee-Konferenz*, in *Villenkolonien*, pp. 96–136.

40. The original German is slightly odd. In the phrase "erfordert die vorherige gemeinsame Behandlung aller an diesen Fragen beteiligten Zentralinstanzen" ("dealing together with all the central bodies involved in these questions"), one would expect the object of "dealing with" (*Behandlung*) to be the questions raised by the Jewish problem. Instead, the grammar makes plain that it is the organizations (*Instanzen*) involved in such questions that need to be dealt with together. Apparently the protocol here misquotes Heydrich's own earlier note from November 29, 1941, and unwittingly reveals his desire to take control of the other authorities.

41. See Eichmann's comments at his trial, session 79, June 12, 1961. A translation can be found at www.nizkor.org/hweb/people/e/eichmann-adolf/transcripts/sessions.

42. ". . . gewisse vorbereitende Arbeiten im Zuge der Endlösung gleich in den betreffenden Gebieten selbst durchzuführen."

43. Kershaw, *Hitler, 1936–1945*, p. 493.

44. Pätzold and Schwarz, *Tagesordnung*, p. 57.

45. Kempner, *Eichmann und Komplizien*, pp. 152–53.

46. Kempner, *Ankläger*, p. 339.

47. Mommsen, "Realization," p. 249; Hans Mommsen, "Aufgabenkreis und Verantwortlichkeit des Staatssekretärs der Reichskanzlei Dr. Wilhelm Kritzinger," *Gutachten*, vol. 2 (Stuttgart: Deutsche Verlags-Anstalt, 1966), p. 381. Dieter Rebentisch, *Führerstaat und Verwaltung im Zweiten Weltkrieg. Verfassungsentwicklung und Verwaltungspolitik 1939–1945* (Franz Steiner Verlag, Stuttgart, 1989), p. 439.

48. My translation from Lösener, "Dokumentation," p. 297.

49. *Trials of War Criminals*, vol. 14, p. 642.

50. Adam, *Judenpolitik*, p. 315.

51. "I would reckon today that it was prepared about two weeks, three weeks, I would reckon today, before the beginning of the

date originally scheduled in December 1941" (Eichmann trial, session 106, July 21, 1961).

52. See Klein, *Wannsee-Konferenz,* p. 5; Scheffler, "Wannsee-Konferenz," p. 24. I am very grateful to Peter Klein for providing additional guidance here, though it seems there is still some ambiguity as to the exact scope of Eichmann's instruction.

53. Originally, Eichmann did, it is true, say that he learned about the plan to murder the Jews around the turn of the year 1941–42. He later not very convincingly backdated his knowledge to summer 1941. What he did not do, however, was place the Wannsee meeting in the context of a major change in Hitler's policy.

54. Peter Longerich, "The Wannsee Conference in the Development of the 'Final Solution,'" Holocaust Educational Trust Research Papers, vol. 1, no. 2, London, 2000, pp. 13–14.

55. The odd note in this context is Bühler and Meyer's appeal for measures to be taken "immediately in the territories concerned." But the statement of their position is so ambiguous that it cannot really influence our conclusions. It may mean that they thought deportations *to* their respective territories should not include too many Jews who could be dealt with before being shipped off.

56. Cited in Hilberg, *Documents of Destruction,* p. 104.

57. See Hilberg, *Perpetrators,* p. 49.

58. This is Mommsen's view, too ("Aufgabenkreis," p. 380). Rebentisch's view that the conference did not make clear what was at stake and that the protocol was purely for internal RSHA purposes I find incomprehensible in view of the protocol's contents, the fact that it was attached to the invitation to subsequent meetings, and Lammers's own early admission of having received it. See Rebentisch, *Führerstaat,* p. 439.

59. Interrogation of Lammers, April 8, 1946, as a witness in the Nuremberg trials; interrogation of Lammers as accused in the Ministries Trial, September 1948; interrogation of Wilhelm Stuckart by his defense attorney in the Ministries Trial, October 6, 1948, all in Pätzold and Schwarz, *Tagesordnung,*

pp. 132, 154, 156–58. On the first occasion, Lammers misremembered the date, referring to a meeting in 1943, but he clearly meant the Wannsee Conference.

60. For this reason, I find untenable John Grenville's interpretation of Wannsee—that the non-Jewish slave reservoir seemed to Heydrich inexhaustible and Jewish labor therefore expendable. See Grenville, "'Endlösung.'"

61. Certainly, there were local variations. In Lodz (in the Warthegau, that is, rather than in the Generalgouvernement) the authorities used the ghetto as a productive enterprise, whereas in the Warsaw ghetto it was only for a brief period in 1941 that a similar approach was adopted. By then, hunger and disease were killing off the ghetto population. See Christopher Browning, "Nazi Ghettoization Policy in Poland," *Path to Genocide,* pp. 28–58.

62. Gerlach, *Kalkulierte Morde,* p. 582.

63. Pohl, *Nationalsozialistische Judenverfolgung,* pp. 165ff.; Sandkühler, *"Endlösung" in Galizien,* p. 134.

64. In fact, of course, the Nazis' murderous approach—as the example of the Generalgouvernement shows—made it impossible to utilize labor rationally. The circle could not be squared in this way. The fact remains, as Yisrael Gutman reminds us, that the few Jews who survived in the camps owed their lives largely to the Germans' need for manpower (Yisrael Gutman, "Auschwitz—An Overview," Gutman and Berenbaum, *Anatomy,* p. 9).

65. Mommsen, "Realization," p. 248.

66. John Grenville is one of a number of historians who have shown that these borderline cases formed the real *policy* content at Wannsee. ("'Endlösung,'" p. 108). See also Jeremy Noakes, "The Development of Nazi Policy towards the German-Jewish 'Mischlinge,'" *Leo Baeck Institute Year Book* 34 (1989): p. 341.

67. Stuckart's testimony is reproduced in Pätzold and Schwarz, *Tagesordnung,* p. 158.

68. Jeremy Noakes, "Wohin gehören die 'Judenmischlinge'? Die Entstehung der ersten Durchführungsverordnungen zu den Nürnberger Gesetzen," *Das Unrechtsregime: Internationale Forschung über den Nationalsozialismus*, ed. Ursula Büttner with Werner Johe and Angelika Voss (Hamburg: Christians Verlag, 1986), pp. 69–89; Hilberg, *Destruction*, vol. 1, pp. 68–74.

69. See Lösener, "Dokumentation," pp. 272, 306. The importance of his role is evidenced by the fact that Interior Ministry policies in which he was not involved were often far closer to those of the party radicals. See the question of half-Jewish youngsters in residential care run by local authorities, in Adam, *Judenpolitik*, pp. 223–24, and Hilberg, *Destruction*, vol. 1, p. 71.

70. See Grenville, "'Endlösung'"; Hilberg, *Destruction*, vol. 2, p. 419, n. 7.

71. Noakes, "'Judenmischlinge,'" p. 69.

72. Hilberg, *Destruction*, vol. 1, p. 70, n. 11.

73. The terms *first degree* and *second degree* entered the legal definition only later.

74. Hilberg, *Destruction*, vol. 1, p. 72.

75. Noakes, "'Judenmischlinge,'" p. 85–86.

76. Noakes, "Development," p. 337; Adam, *Judenpolitik*, p. 218; Meyer, *"Jüdische Mischlinge,"* pp. 30–31.

77. See report by Fred K. Salter from the U.S. Consulate General, reproduced in *The Judicial System and the Jews in Nazi Germany*, vol. 13 of *The Holocaust: Selected Documents in Eighteen Volumes*, ed. John Mendelsohn (New York: Garland, 1982), pp. 1–32.

78. Noakes, "Development," p. 339; Lösener, "Dokumentation," p. 297.

79. Grenville, "'Endlösung,'" pp. 109–10.

80. Meyer, *"Jüdische Mischlinge,"* p. 25.

81. Hilberg, *Destruction*, vol. 2, p. 418.

82. Scheffler, "Wannsee-Konferenz," pp. 18, 23, 26; Walter Hagen, *Die Geheime Front* (Vienna, 1950), p. 24, cited in Gerald

Reitlinger, *The Final Solution: The Attempt to Exterminate the Jews of Europe, 1939–1945* (London: Valentine Mitchell, 1953, 1961), p. 550, n. 10; Jäckel, "On the Purpose," p. 45; Reitlinger, *Final Solution*, p. 102.

83. Scheffler, "Wannsee-Konferenz," p. 18; Reitlinger, *Final Solution*, p. 102.

84. Eichmann's testimony, June 1, 1960, in Pätzold and Schwarz, *Tagesordnung*, pp. 162–63.

85. Jäckel, "On the Purpose," p. 45.

86. My translation from Tuchel, *Am grossen Wannsee*, p. 121.

87. Witte et al., *Dienstkalender*, p. 265.

88. Witte et al., *Dienstkalender*, p. 274.

89. Witte et al., *Dienstkalender*, p. 277.

90. Eichmann trial, session 78, June 23, 1961; see n. 41 above.

91. Safrian, *Eichmann-Männer*, pp. 143–47, esp. p. 146.

92. Hilberg, *Perpetrators*, pp. 48–49.

93. George C. Browder, *Foundations of the Nazi Police State: The Formation of SIPO and SD* (Lexington: University Press of Kentucky, 1990), p. 229; Lösener, "Dokumentation," p. 286.

94. Hilberg, *Documents of Destruction*, p. 104.

95. Cited in Gerlach, "Wannsee Conference," p. 129.

96. Eichmann trial, session 10, April 19, 1961.

97. Pätzold, *Judenmord*, pp. 201ff.

98. Pätzold, *Judenmord*, pp. 201ff.; Helmut Ortner, *Der Hinrichter: Roland Freisler—Mörder im Dienste Hitlers* (Vienna: Zsolnay Verlag, 1993), pp. 51, 60.

99. Robert Wistrich, *Who's Who in Nazi Germany* (London: Weidenfeld and Nicolson, 1982), p. 310; Herbert, *Best*, pp. 284–85; *Trials of War Criminals*, vol. 14, pp. 631–32; Rebentisch, *Führerstaat*, pp. 109, 545.

100. Rebentisch, *Führerstaat*, p. 318.

101. Freisler, Meyer, and Stuckart were in the first group, Bühler, Schöngarth, and Leibbrandt in the second (Pätzold and Schwarz, *Tagesordnung*, pp. 201ff.).

102. Herbert, *Best*, p. 285.

103. Herbert, *Best*, p. 284.
104. On Freisler's degree of antisemitism, see H. W. Koch, *In the Name of the Volk: Political Justice in Hitler's Germany* (London: I. B. Tauris, 1989), p. 31.
105. Ortner, *Hinrichter*, p. 101.
106. Browder, *Foundations*, p. 185.
107. "Politische Beurteilung des Kriminal-Oberinspektors Heinrich Müller durch die Gauleitung München-Oberbayeren, Amt für Beamte, 4.1.1937," signed Otto Nippold, Deputy Gauleiter, Münich-Oberbayern; quoted in Aronson, *Reinhard Heydrich*, p. 321.
108. Browning, *Final Solution*, p. 27.
109. Browning, *Final Solution*, p. 28; Reitlinger, *Final Solution*, p. 24.
110. E.g., on Madagascar. See Browning, *Final Solution;* Steur, *Theodor Dannecker.*
111. Herbert, *Best*, pp. 285–86.
112. The Nuremberg judges (see *Trials of War Criminals*, vol. 14, p. 645) were, however, wrong in assuming that Stuckart wrote in 1938 that, after the Nuremberg Laws and subsequent codifications, racial legislation was "essentially complete." Stuckart did indeed write that "many of the decisions" already taken would "lose their importance as the final solution of the Jewish problem" was reached. But these words do not appear in the 1938 edition of his legal handbook, *The Care for Race and Heredity in the Legislation of the Reich*, and were added only in the 1943 edition. I am grateful to Hans-Christian Jasch for pointing this out.
113. See Helmut Grosscurth's comments in *Tagebücher eines Abwehroffiziers, 1938–1940* (Stuttgart: Deutsche Verlags-Anstalt, 1970), p. 162. See also the comments of Heinz Höhne, cited in Deschner, *Reinhard Heydrich*, p. 174.
114. Aronson, *Reinhard Heydrich*, pp. 244–54.
115. Rebentisch, *Führerstaat*, p. 544.
116. Mommsen, "Aufgabenkreis," p. 370.

117. Mommsen, "Aufgabenkreis," p. 389.
118. *Trials of War Criminals,* vol. 14, p. 643.
119. Mommsen, "Aufgabenkreis," p. 386.
120. Rebentisch, *Führerstaat,* p. 436.
121. Lösener, "Dokumentation."
122. Fleming, *Hitler and the Final Solution,* pp. 70–71.
123. Safrian, *Eichmann-Männer,* p. 149.
124. Ronald Headland, *Messages of Murder: A Study of the Reports of the Einsatzgruppen of the Security Police and the Security Service* (Madison: Fairleigh Dickinson University Press, 1992), pp. 46–47, 230.
125. Browning, *Final Solution,* pp. 73–74.
126. *Trials of War Criminals,* vol. 14, p. 423.
127. *Trials of War Criminals,* vol. 14, p. 640.
128. Lösener, "Dokumentation," p. 311.
129. Gerlach, *Kalkulierte Morde,* pp. 544–45.
130. Safrian, *Eichmann-Männer,* p. 142.
131. Pohl, *"Judenpolitik,"* p. 94.
132. Browning, *Final Solution,* p. 64.
133. Browning, *Final Solution,* pp. 56ff.

5. A LARGELY SUCCESSFUL DAY

1. Hilberg, *Destruction,* vol. 2, p. 491.
2. Meyer, *"Jüdische Mischlinge,"* p. 98.
3. Testimony reproduced in Pätzold and Schwarz, *Tagesordnung,* p. 156.
4. Hilberg, *Destruction,* vol. 2, p. 420, n. 9; Adam, *Judenpolitik,* p. 323, n. 100; Meyer, *"Jüdische Mischlinge,"* pp. 98, 404, n. 16.
5. Lösener, "Dokumentation," p. 298.
6. See Meyer, *"Jüdische Mischlinge,"* p. 98.
7. Aly and Heim, *Vordenker der Vernichtung,* p. 418.
8. Minutes of consultation with Lammers on October 2, 1941, in Mendelsohn, *Legalizing the Holocaust: The Later Phase, 1939–1943,* vol. 2 of *The Holocaust,* pp. 284–86. See also Hilberg, *Destruction,* vol. 2, pp. 418, 420, n. 9.

9. Eichmann trial, session 79, June 26, 1961; session 107, July 24, 1961.
10. So-called Sassen interviews, cited in the Eichmann trial, session 75, June 20, 1961.
11. Eichmann trial, session 79, June 26, 1961; session 106, July 21, 1961.
12. See also Aly and Heim, *Vordenker der Vernichtung*, p. 469.
13. Aly and Heim, *Vordenker der Vernichtung*, p. 470.
14. Kempner, *Eichmann und Komplizien*, p. 165; Noakes, "Development," p. 343.
15. Himmler's letter to Gottlob Berger, quoted in Noakes, "Development," p. 346.
16. The complete minutes of the March and October meetings are reproduced in Kempner, *Eichmann und Komplizien*, pp. 165–80, 255–67. See also the note on the March meeting by Franz Rademacher, reproduced in abbreviated form in Pätzold and Schwarz, *Tagesordnung*, p. 119. The full text is in the Wiener Library, London, document K195.
17. The Justice Ministry's objections are not identified in the minutes but are referred to by Rademacher in his subsequent note of March 7 (Wiener Library, document K195). See Hilberg, *Destruction*, vol. 2, pp. 421–29, and Noakes's more generous interpretation in "Development," p. 347.
18. At Nuremberg, Lammers's position was not believed; see prosecution summing up the Ministries Trial, reproduced in Mendelsohn, *The Ohlendorf and Weizsaecker Cases*, vol. 18 of *The Holocaust*, p. 106. But the discovery of a memo from Schlegelberger has vindicated Lammers on this issue. See Schlegelberger memo in Bundesarchiv file R22/52, cited on David Irving's Web site, www.fpp.co.uk/Himmler/Schlegelberger/DocItself0342.html. Irving interprets the memo as meaning Hitler rejected the Final Solution as a whole. This is inconsistent not only with Hitler's own remarks but also with his demonstrated ability to stop developments he did not like.
19. Meyer, *"Jüdische Mischlinge,"* p. 12.

20. Noakes, "Development," pp. 347–48; Meyer, *"Jüdische Misch-linge,"* p. 51.

21. Adler, *Verwaltete Mensch,* pp. 202ff., 280–81.

22. Wolfgang Benz, "Die Dimension des Völkermords," *Dimension des Völkermords: Die Zahl der jüdischen Opfer des National-sozialismus* (Munich: Oldenbourg Verlag, 1991), p. 17.

23. Browning, *Path to Genocide,* p. ix.

24. Letter from Heydrich, January 25, 1942, reproduced on the Web site of the Gedenkstätte Haus der Wannsee Konferenz, (www.ghwk.de/deut/chefsd.htm).

25. My translation from Tuchel, *Am grossen Wannsee,* p. 121; see also Gerlach, "Wannsee Conference," p. 130.

26. Wisliceny's postwar testimony gains some credibility because of his earlier exchanges with Rudolf Kastner in Hungary before the end of the war. See Kempner, *Eichmann und Komplizien,* p. 182, and Ernest Landau, ed., *Der Kastner-Berich* (Munich: Kindler Verlag, 1961), passim.

27. Eichmann trial, session 10, April 19, 1961; see also Gerlach, "Wannsee Conference," p. 111.

28. Kempner, *Eichmann und Komplizien,* p. 148.

29. Kempner, *Eichmann und Komplizien,* p. 148; Gerlach, *Kalku-lierte Morde,* p. 755.

30. Eichmann trial, session 79, June 26, 1961.

31. Safrian, *Eichmann-Männer,* p. 174.

32. Cited in Kempner, *Eichmann und Komplizien,,* p. 180.

33. My translation of quotation in Aly and Heim, *Vordenker der Vernichtung,* p. 460.

34. The invitation, sent out on February 26, is reproduced in Kempner, *Eichmann und Komplizien,* p. 150.

35. The cover note with the Wannsee protocol is dated February 26, 1942 and it seems the recipients received their copies in early March; Foreign Office, at least, received its copy on March 2, 1942 (Kempner, *Eichmann und Komplizien,* p. 149).

36. Pohl, *"Judenpolitik,"* p. 109.

37. Pohl, *"Judenpolitik,"* pp. 102, 110.

38. Gerlach, "Wannsee Conference," p. 133; Gerlach, *Kalkulierte Morde*, p. 755.
39. Pohl, *Nationalsozialistische Judenverfolgung*, p. 204.
40. Longerich, *Politik der Vernichtung*, p. 488; Yitzhak Arad, *Belzec, Sobibor, Treblinka: The Operation Reinhard Death Camps* (Bloomington: Indiana University Press, 1987), pp. 75, 81, 392; Christopher Browning, "A Final Hitler Decision for the 'Final Solution'? The Riegner Telegram Reconsidered," *Holocaust and Genocide Studies* 10 (1996): pp. 3–10.
41. Witte, "Two Decisions," p. 333–34. See also Witte et al., *Dienstkalender*, pp. 67, 73; Pohl, *Nationalsozialistische Judenverfolgung*, pp. 204–05; Browning, "Final Hitler Decision"; Orth, "Rudolf Höss," p. 48; Pohl, *"Judenpolitik,"* pp. 128; Gerlach, *Kalkulierte Morde*, p. 662ff.
42. Eichmann had by this time in the trial shifted from his earlier position that the Final Solution was ordered at the end of the year to the view that the order had originated in the summer of 1941.
43. Eichmann trial, session 93, July 12, 1961.
44. Herbert, *Best*, p. 320.

ACKNOWLEDGMENTS

I am indebted to all who provided helpful comments and suggestions or engaged with me in valuable discussions, especially Hans-Christian Jasch, Norbert Kampe, and Peter Klein, as well as Volker Berghahn, David Cesarani, Richard Evans, Christian Gerlach, Peter Longerich, Nicholas Stargardt, Klaus-Dieter Schmidt (the translator for the German edition), and Peter Witte. If this phalanx of experts has failed to remove all errors from the present account, that is my fault, not theirs. The staff at the Wiener Library, London, and the Haus der Wannsee-Konferenz (the Museum of the Wannsee Conference) in Berlin were extremely helpful in providing materials. Interested readers may consult the museum's many resources at www.ghwk.de. I am also very grateful to Simon Winder of Penguin, whose original project this was, and to Peter Robinson of Curtis Brown for his role in shaping it. For the U.S. edition, my many thanks to Sara Bershtel and her assistant, Shara Kay, as well as to my copy editor, Roslyn Schloss. Some of the time writing this book was spent as a guest of Michigan State University, and it's my pleasure to acknowledge the hospitality I received there, with particular thanks to Norman Graham, Dagmar Herzog, Steve Weiland, and Conni Zellar. I am grateful also to the University of Southampton for allowing me the time to write the book. My biggest debt is to Ann Larabee—for our many helpful discussions, for crucial advice, particularly in the closing stages of writing, and for providing the emotional center that made writing possible. This book is dedicated to her.

INDEX

Index

77, 83, 86, 89, 90, 106, 151, 152,
153
European Jews, 55–56, 57, 101
German Jews, 65–66, 74–77, 101,
125
Heydrich and, 120, 134
and killing, 72, 73, 107, 108–9
Mischlinge, 119
plans for, 92
resumption of, 70, 91
to Soviet Union, 110
transition from, to murder, 112,
155–56
Wannsee Conference and, 149–50
deportees
killing of, 70–72, 75–76, 138
treatment of, 74–77, 125
Deutscher Hochschulring, 23, 129
Dieckmann, Christoph, 8
divorce, compulsory, 147
Dühring, Eugen, 11

East
evacuation of Jews to, 58, 87, 88,
100–2, 104, 109, 126
Eastern Galicia, 62–63
Eichmann, Adolf, 29, 31, 64, 85, 109,
118, 132, 146
and deportations, 38, 66
and genocide, 134
and reservation plan, 32
trial and testimony, 52, 54–55, 96–
98, 100, 102–3, 104, 107–8, 110,
120–21, 122, 124, 126, 138–39,
143–45, 153–54
and Wannsee Conference, 80–81,
96–97, 148–50, 156
Einsatzgruppen, 34, 36, 39–40, 41, 43–
44, 64, 71, 113, 137
guidelines for, 134
killing operations, 46–47, 138,
139
Einsatzkommandos, 40, 44, 96, 112, 123,
139
emigration, 12–14, 19, 21, 25, 28, 32–
33, 89–90, 132, 134
to Palestine, 74
prohibited, 72

promoting, 106
stopped, 57, 99–100
European Jews, 26, 155
deportation of, 55, 57, 101
Hitler's decision to murder, 107
killing of, 48–50, 51, 52, 87, 89
eradication of, 72, 111, 121, 149,
152
euthanasia, 27, 35, 52, 90
evacuation, 4, 58, 88, 100–2, 104,
105–6, 108, 109, 119, 126
of *Mischlinge*, 146
extermination, 9–12, 91, 113
policy of, 91
extermination camps, 4, 52, 54, 68,
110, 155

Feldscher, Werner, 85
final solution, 3, 8, 19, 54–55, 111,
144
in Generalgouvernement, 106, 141
meaning of, 111
most intense phase of, 153
plan for, 5–6, 148–49, 150–51, 156
Wannsee Conference/Protocol and,
99, 100, 101, 104, 105, 114, 121
First World War, 10, 11, 79
Germany's defeat in, 23, 27
Foreign Office, 1, 83, 85, 86, 95, 131,
132, 139
German Department, 138
Four Year Plan, 19, 82, 95, 103, 135
France, 57, 101
Frank, Hans, 30–31, 32, 37, 38, 55, 56,
66–67, 68, 84, 95, 122, 123, 128
diary, 110
meeting with Hitler, 141
speech on Jews, 87–88
Freisler, Roland, 95, 128, 130
Frick, Wilhelm, 96, 145
Friedländer, Saul, 7
Fritsch, General, 22

gas/gassing, 3, 35, 48, 52, 63–64, 72,
109, 110, 151, 153
Hitler on, 10, 11, 12
experiments with, 59, 71
mass murder through, 152

Index

Index

and *Mischlinge*, 146, 147
and mass murder, 63–64, 138
personnel changes in Generalgouvernement, 151
resettlement program, 30, 31, 33
and SS, 19–20
and transition to genocide, 69, 70, 72, 73, 75, 76, 77–78
Wannsee Conference as campaign to assert supremacy, 121–24, 125
Hitler, Adolf, 3, 5, 7, 80, 82, 135, 141, 148
agenda of, 25–28
ambiguity, 6, 12–14, 73, 89–90
antisemitism, 10, 12, 17, 69–70
authority of, 17–18, 70, 91, 156
citizenship and blood laws, 115
decision by, 48–51, 107, 108
declared war on U.S., 86, 87, 89, 91
and deportations, 38, 39, 56–61, 65–66, 109
genocide, 40–41, 42, 44–46, 47, 59, 84
and henchmen, 15–25
Himmler's meetings with, 152, 153
on Jewish citizenship, 136
and Jewish question, 26, 31, 49–50, 70, 87, 88
and *Mischlinge* issue, 147
and murder, 31, 33, 34, 35–36, 41, 49–50
prophecy, 26–27, 50, 70, 73, 87
rhetoric of extermination, 9–12, 49–50, 70
sensitivity to public morale, 116, 125
setting the tone, 35–36, 44–45, 133
and transition to genocide, 69–70, 73, 74, 77, 78, 90, 91
Hitler Youth, 12–13
Hofmann, Otto, 95–96, 102, 105, 142
Holocaust, 4, 5, 7–8, 11, 39, 50, 148
Höppner, Rolf Neinz, 64–65
Höss, Rudolf, 52, 54

ideology, 7, 12, 21, 22, 34, 40
and bureaucracy, 41
in state apparatus, 133–34
in transition to genocide, 130

Institute for Research on the Jewish Question, 118

Jäckel, Eberhard, 3, 92, 120
Jäger, Karl, 39
Japan, 84, 88
Jeckeln, Friedrich, 75
Jewish policy, 14, 15–16, 19
Jewish problem, 9, 40, 45–46, 132
proposals for dealing with, 64–65
Jewish question, 34, 53, 62, 150
centralizing initiatives on, 122–24
final solution, 3, 144 (*see also* final solution)
in Generalgouvernement, 141–42
Heydrich and, 21, 134
Hitler and, 26, 31, 49–50, 70, 87, 88
ministries responsible for, 83, 95–96, 97
players in, 19–25
responsbility for, 125
Rosenberg on, 88–89
in Wannsee Conference, 81, 82, 84, 86, 99, 103, 105, 121
war and, 28–29
Jews, 2, 18, 83
deaths of, 39, 40, 41
defining, 114–20
discriminatory measures against, 12–14, 15, 22, 41
elimination/extermination, 37, 50–51, 52, 63, 68–69, 72–73, 74, 132, 137, 148
evacuation to East, 58, 88, 100–2, 104, 109, 126
half/quarter, 2, 4, 17, 102, 114, 115–17, 118, 137, 146
in Hitler's rhetoric, 9, 10, 12
as hostages, 27, 60, 61–62, 73–74, 91
suspected of international conspiracy, 25–28
killing, 35, 89, 137–38, 148
killing: in Wannsee Protocol, 104–13
mixed-race, 84, 85–86, 124
Nazi action against, 99–100
problems of food and epidemics, 65

Index

Jews (*cont.*)
  resettlement, 33–34
  working/not working, 71, 106
  see also deportation(s), European Jews;
    genocide; German Jews; Soviet
    Jews
"Jews Are Guilty, The" (Goebbels), 72–
  73

Katzmann, Fritz, 63, 113, 151
Kaufmann, Karl, 57
Kempner, Robert, 2, 82, 105
Kershaw, Ian, 7
killing
  acceptability of, 56, 61
  knowledge of, 137–38
  means of, 109–11
Klein, Peter, 8
Klopfer, Gerhard, 95, 129, 130, 136,
  137
Koeppen, Werner, 60
Kommissarbefehl, 41
Koppe, Wilhelm, 70
Kovno, 74, 75, 76, 125
Kristallnacht, 13, 14, 16, 18, 19, 21, 132
Kritzinger, Friedrich-Wilhelm, 95, 105,
  110, 111, 134–35, 136
Krüger, Friedrich-Wilhelm, 84, 85,
  122, 123, 151, 153
Krumey, Hermann, 149
Kube, Wilhelm, 66, 76–77
Küchler, Georg von, 36
Kvaternik, Slavko, 55, 74

Lammers, Heinrich, 98, 111, 126, 135,
  136, 143, 147
Lange, Rudolf, 75, 96, 123, 129, 139
Leibbrandt, Georg, 95, 128, 129
Liebermann, Max, 93
Lipski, Jozef, 26
Lodz, 60, 65, 66, 70–71, 74–75, 109,
  152
Lohse, Hinrich, 72, 123
Longerich, Peter, 7, 108–9, 152
Lösener, Bernhard, 77, 105, 115, 119,
  121, 125, 138, 142, 143
Lublin, 37, 67–69, 151, 152, 153, 155
Luther, Martin, 86, 95, 102, 124, 131–
  32, 139

Madagascar, 31, 35, 55
Manoschek, Walter, 62
manpower shortages, 112–13, 114, 155
Marr, Wilhelm, 11
mass murder, 4, 8, 28, 34, 59, 150,
  152–53
  of deportees, 125
  knowledge of, 138–39
  transition to genocide, 48–78
Mein Kampf (Hitler), 9, 10, 11
mentally ill, 34, 35, 64
Meyer, Alfred, 95, 103–4, 127–28, 129
ministries, 19, 114
  Nazi Party members in, 127–29
  and killing, 136–38
  responsible for Jewish question, 83,
    95–96, 97
  Wannsee Conference and, 122–24
Ministry for the Occupied Eastern Territories, 72, 83, 85, 95, 112–13,
  123, 125, 127, 137, 143–46
Ministry of Justice, 83, 84, 95, 128, 147
Ministry of Propaganda, 83, 94–95,
  127, 147
Ministry of the Interior, 17, 20, 83,
  85–86, 95, 96, 114, 115, 121,
  128, 133
  knowledge of mass murders, 138
  and *Mischlinge*, 142
  policy toward Jews, 135, 136
  protection of half-Jews, 116
  relationship with RSHA, 123–24
  subordinate to Himmler, 145, 146
Minoux, Friedrich, 93–94, 96
Minsk, 59, 66, 71, 74, 75, 76, 83, 109,
  139, 149
Mischlinge, 84, 102, 116, 117, 118–19,
  135, 136, 140, 142–43, 145, 146,
  156
mixed marriages, 84, 102, 105, 114,
  117, 119, 135, 137, 142, 143,
  146–48
Mommsen, Hans, 7, 16, 105, 113, 135
Müller, Heinrich, 96, 130–31, 132,
  134, 137–38, 145, 147
murder, 32–37, 48–49, 70, 71–72, 90
  deportation replaced by, 112
  of deportees, 75–76
  discussed at Wannsee, 144

Index

extending, 51–56
machinery of, 59
middle managers of, 61–69
Nazi system of, 4
plans for, 92
transition from deportations to, 112, 155–56
Wannsee Protocol blueprint for, 4
see also genocide; mass murder

National Socialism, 22, 24
National Socialist Welfare, 93
nationalism, 22, 23, 24, 127–28, 130
Nazi Party/Nazis, 4, 5, 6, 17, 18, 22, 25, 37, 87
  antisemitism, 14, 21, 36
  attitudes to Jewish labor, 111–13
  and deportations, 31–32
  Jewish policy, 14, 114
  records destroyed by, 4
  system of murder, 4, 28
  Wannsee Conference participants, 93, 127–29, 131
  and war, 91
Nazi Women's League, 93
Nebe, Arthur, 64
Neumann, Erich, 95, 103, 134–35
New York Jews, 88, 89
Night of the Long Knives, 23, 34
Ninth Fort, 75
Nuremberg Laws, 16, 17, 115, 116, 117, 118
Nuremberg trials, 1, 90, 93, 104–5, 106, 111, 135, 142, 147

Operation Barbarossa, 31, 41, 43, 57–58

Party Chancellery, 83, 84, 95, 118
Pearl Harbor, 86
Pohl, Dieter, 8
Pokorny, Adolf, 143
Poland, 2, 8, 26, 28, 39, 41, 64, 134
  civilian administration in, 33, 36, 37–38, 127, 128
  extermination camps, 54, 110
  final solution to begin in, 103
  Jewish question in, 123
  mass executions in, 34

murders in, 35–36
police empire in, 67
representative at Wannsee Conference, 84
sending Jews to, 29–31, 33–34, 58
treatment of Jews in, 37
Polish Jews, 3, 29, 30, 66, 67, 69, 152, 155
Pripet Marshes, 46, 56, 73

race questions, 83, 95–96, 119
Racial Policy Office, 118
Rademacher, Franz, 31, 139
Raeder, Erich, 31
Rath, Ernst von, 18
Rebentisch, Dieter, 105
Reich Association of Jews, 107
Reich Central Office for Jewish Emigration, 21, 99
Reich Chancellery, 83, 95, 105, 135–36, 138, 143, 147
Reich Security Main Office (RSHA), 5, 14, 20, 24, 38, 85, 97, 98, 114, 118, 130, 131, 136, 139, 147
  breakthroughs at Wannsee Conference, 141–42, 143
  Jewish section, 29, 81
  leading role of, 121, 123–24, 125, 126, 133, 134
  mastery in Jewish question, 120, 145
  and resettlement program, 31
Reichssicherheitshauptam, 80
Reichstag, 27, 86, 87
Reitlinger, Gerald, 132
reservation, 26, 27, 29, 32–33, 56, 73, 77, 109
  abandoning idea of, 114
  bridge from, to genocide, 113
resettlement, 33–34
Ribbentrop, Joachim von, 131
Riga, 71, 74, 77, 83
  deportations to, 123, 124–25, 138
  killing of Jews in, 75–76, 139
Romania, 26, 100
Roosevelt, Franklin D., 73–74, 91
Rosenberg, Alfred, 24, 44, 45, 53, 54, 58, 60, 72, 88–89, 90, 91, 121, 127, 129

209

Index

Index

ABOUT THE AUTHOR

The author of *A Past in Hiding* and a winner of the Fraenkel Prize in contemporary history and the *Jewish Quarterly*'s Wingate Literary Prize, MARK ROSEMAN teaches modern history at the University of Southampton and is a member of the German History Society. A graduate of Cambridge University, he has published widely in English- and German-language publications on many aspects of twentieth-century German history. He lives in Southampton, England.